THE BAY TREE™

HOME
DELI
RECIPES

THE BAY TREE™

HOME DELI RECIPES

The Secrets of Delicious Cooking
with Great Deli Ingredients

EMMA MACDONALD

To Mal With love Emma

dbp

DUNCAN BAIRD PUBLISHERS

LONDON

To my parents for the delicious meals they prepared for us as children, and their early inspiration and encouragement to follow my passion for food. And more latterly to my husband and three wonderful sons who regularly endure experimental suppers and assist me in making endless batches of soups and preserves.

Home Deli Recipes
Emma Macdonald

First published in the United Kingdom and Ireland in 2013 by
Duncan Baird Publishers, an imprint of
Watkins Publishing Limited
Sixth Floor
75 Wells Street
London W1T 3QH

A member of Osprey Group

Managing Editor: Grace Cheetham
Editor: Emma Clegg
Recipe Tester: Nicola Graimes
Managing Designer: Suzanne Tuhrim
Commissioned photography: Toby Scott, except on pages 69, 70, 129, 173 and 219 by William Lingwood
Food Stylist: Jayne Cross, except on pages 69, 70, 129, 173 and 219 by Bridget Sargeson
Prop Stylist: Lucy Harvey
Commissioned artwork: Jade Wheaton
Picture Research: Emma Copestake
Production: Uzma Taj

A CIP record for this book is available from the British Library

ISBN: 978-1-84899-109-5

1 3 5 7 9 10 8 6 4 2

Typeset in Du Turner and Rockwell
Colour reproduction by PDQ, UK
Printed in China

Notes on the Recipes
Unless otherwise stated:
Use medium eggs, fruit and vegetables
Use fresh ingredients, including herbs and chillies
Do not mix metric and imperial measurements
1 tsp = 5ml   1 tbsp = 15ml   1 cup = 250ml

Publisher's note: While every care has been taken in compiling the recipes for this book, Watkins Publishing Limited, or any other persons who have been involved in working on this publication, cannot accept responsibility for any errors or omissions, inadvertent or not, that may be found in the recipes or text, nor for any problems that may arise as a result of preparing one of these recipes. If you are pregnant or breastfeeding or have any special dietary requirements or medical conditions, it is advisable to consult a medical professional before following any of the recipes contained in this book.

Contents

FOREWORD

After almost 20 years in the food business a great wish of mine has been to publish my own cookery book – and now here is *Home Deli Recipes*, a collection of my favourite deli secrets, and so much more.

From the age of thirteen I wanted to make a career out of cooking and I spent much of my free time devising new recipes and baking cakes for friends and family. I studied catering at college and, after leaving, worked as an apprentice in a number of restaurants in France before then travelling through Asia, working in various restaurants and catering establishments as I went. This was a great way of learning to appreciate different cultures, ingredients and styles of cooking. In Asia, I discovered the eclectic mix of spices sold in markets and how they were used in cooking, along with the techniques that make the Asian cuisine so fresh and vibrant. This has influenced my own style of cooking, especially in the way I like to add a fresh interpretation to classic recipes in our Bay Tree condiments.

I grew up in a house where there was always a supply of home-made jams and chutneys, so it seemed a natural progression to start making my own, and in time I decided to make a living from it. I established The Bay Tree Food Co. in my early twenties, producing traditional, home cooked condiments and marmalades with a modern twist. More recently, we have moved into creating home-style cook-in sauces and pasta sauces. One of our greatest early successes was Aga-dried tomatoes, but unfortunately the demand far outweighed the volume we could make at the time, so we then set our sights on what could be done without sacrificing our wish to create high-quality products with no artificial additives.

It hasn't always been plain sailing, and I quickly found that making products in a jar with a decent shelf life (as opposed to making a meal to be eaten straight away) requires a certain amount of food science, but this aspect has also always fascinated me. Recognizing and appreciating that fresh produce can vary in taste, texture or colour, depending on the season, weather or growing conditions, and using this knowledge, can make such a big difference to the end product. I always make products as close as I can to the home-cooked equivalent without compromising on flavour and texture or having to add artificial additives, while also offering the convenience of a product with a good shelf life.

The recipes in this book – like The Bay Tree products – are predominantly based on a traditional theme but with an exciting twist. My recipe for gravadlax (see page 56), for instance, features fresh root ginger and lemon to flavour the salmon, instead of the more classic dill. I also hope you'll have a go at making pâtés, preserves, sauces and even some home smoking. If this doesn't appeal, there are also recipes that use these ingredients bought ready-made from a deli to suit those times when you want to knock up a mouth-watering meal. Some recipes are simple and others demand more effort, but either way the end results are worth it!

I've also included recipes for some of our popular Bay Tree products such as Piccalilli (see page 138), which is adapted from a traditional recipe but with a little extra something to perk it up. While piccalilli is excellent served with a meat or cheese platter, I also wanted to show how it can be used as part of a meal, in this case remoulade (see page 139). You can also create this recipe with a shop-bought piccalilli. Home-made condiments, jams and sauces are such a treat to have in the kitchen and are a delight to give to family and friends. The fact that they are so appreciated and enjoyed makes the effort more worthwhile.

I hope you'll enjoy these recipes and find the time to be creative with making the deli products, as well as using the ready-made ones in the recipes.

COOKING THE BAY TREE WAY

A good deli is a fantastic treasure trove of culinary delights, from cured meats, smoked fish and sweet preserves to farmhouse cheeses, fresh pasta and hand-raised pies.

This book is designed to be both accessible and inspiring, featuring a collection of recipes for dishes that incorporate ready-made deli foods and also more challenging recipes showing how you can create your own deli products at home, such as home-cured bacon, ricotta, fresh pasta, flavoured vinegar, seafood pâté and artisan breads. There are also suggestions on how to give classic deli foods an interesting new spin, such as a crab terrine that forms the filling of a creamy seafood tart (see page 49), or a recipe for home-smoked chicken breast that gives a delicious subtle smokiness to a classic paella (see page 29), or a garlic and fennel mustard that makes a flavoursome crust for a roasted leg of lamb (see page 123). So whether you buy your deli products ready-made or make them from scratch, there's no doubting there's a wonderful variety from which to choose. Enjoy exploring them within these pages.

MEAT & POULTRY

While the French term "charcuterie" may traditionally just cover pork, it has become a generic word encompassing all manner of cured and preserved meats from all over the world. Pork still reigns supreme in the world of charcuterie, however, thanks to its incredible versatility: just think pâtés, terrines, bacon, salami, sausages, ham and pies.

Arguably the finest and most expensive ham is the Spanish jamón Ibérico. The Ibérico pig roams freely and spends its final months in oak forests feeding on acorns (bellota), which give the meat a unique delicate, sweet flavour. The curing process that follows takes at least 12 months, and up to 36 months, to produce a ham with melt-in-the-mouth qualities. Salt curing draws out the moisture in meat, which intensifies the flavour and firms up the texture. It also inhibits the growth of harmful bacteria. You can try salt curing with the recipe for Home-Cured Bacon (see page 22), which is immensely satisfying and rewarding to make.

Game – both feathered and furred – is becoming more widely available and is enjoying a resurgence in popularity. Rabbit, pheasant, partridge, pigeon and venison are perfect for pies, pâtés, terrines and potted meats, but as they are low in fat you may need to combine them with a fattier meat, such as duck or pork, to keep them moist. It's this generous fat content that makes duck and pork perfect for rillettes, potted meat, confit and pâtés. When you're making meat pâtés, try duck, goose and chicken livers, which are not expensive to buy and create a great base flavour.

FISH & SHELLFISH

Fish and shellfish can be smoked, salted, cured or pickled, but if you intend to preserve your own seafood, the key is to use the freshest you can buy.

Home smoking is growing in popularity and is easy to do, and the Home-Smoked Trout (see page 68) is a great starting point. This is hot smoked, which cooks the food while imparting a delicate smokiness. You don't need any special equipment; I use an old wok, but a sturdy biscuit tin, or galvanized dustbin if smoking on a larger scale outdoors, can be used, or you could invest in a purpose-built hot smoker.

In contrast, cold smoking is a much longer, slower process and does not cook the food. However, cold smoking does lend a much more intense smokiness than hot smoking and it also extends the shelf life of a product through preserving it. Cold smoking does also require investment in specialist large pieces of smoking equipment, which makes it out of bounds for most home cooks. Cold-smoked salmon is probably the most popular fish for smoking, but look, too, for halibut, sea bass and haddock, which are delicious when sliced very thinly and served on rye bread with a spoonful of cucumber pickle. Other smoky delights include smoked mussels, kippers, taramasalata and smoked eels.

Herring and mackerel that have been pickled, brined, marinated or soused (meaning cooked or raw fish that have been soaked in a flavoured light white wine or vinegar marinade-cum-dressing) are a familiar sight on the deli counter and are also sold in jars. They make convenient canapés or a tasty light lunch served on Scandinavian crispbread with a spoonful of soured cream and a sprig of dill, chopped finely and stirred into a potato salad, or cut into paper-thin slices and served with a mustard mayo and a crisp green salad.

When it comes to anchovies, we tend to love them or hate them! This small fish, belonging to the herring family, is sold in many forms: whole, filleted, salted, brined, in oil, in vinegar and/or flavoured with chilli, spices or herbs. If you want to tame any saltiness, first soak the anchovies in milk or water and then pat them dry. Usually found on top of pizzas or in salade Niçoise, anchovies are also used to make numerous variations of a sauce-cum-dip, including the gutsy French anchoïade, the Italian bagna càuda, the Provençal tapenade and the quintessentially English *Patum Peperium* or Gentleman's Relish.

DAIRY & CHEESE

Milk is at the heart of all things dairy, whether from a cow, sheep or goat, and it is incredibly versatile. Yogurt is a cultured milk product that is a common ingredient in both cooked and uncooked dishes. I like to use a lighter, fresher yogurt in Indian raitas, salad dressings or in baking, while the richer, creamier alternatives, particularly Greek yogurt from ewe's milk, work well in sauces or in desserts.

Cream also comes in many guises. Single cream is great for pouring over desserts or fruit, while double cream is best used in cooking as it is less likely to split when heated due to its higher fat content. Even though double cream can be whipped, whipping cream is lower in fat and is perfect for filling cakes and pastries and for spooning over desserts. For the best results, always make sure the bowl and whisk are cold before whisking.

This book includes recipes for Labneh (see page 78) and a Rich Home-made Ricotta (see page 218). These fresh, mild cheeses are a great starting point for cheese-making and it's worth experimenting with adding different flavourings such as herbs and spices.

The next step on from making fresh cheese is to add rennet, which encourages milk to separate into curds and whey. After this separation process, the curds are salted and pressed into cheese, and they are then matured or ripened. This is an ultra-simplistic description of how to make this wonderful food product, and there are many thousands of types of cheese, each with their own nuances, which are influenced by not only the cheese-making process but also the source of the milk.

Whichever type of cheese you choose, it is always best to serve it at room temperature when the flavour is allowed to come to the fore and the texture starts to yield.

STORE-CUPBOARD CONDIMENTS

A well-stocked store cupboard is a wondrous thing. Shelves laden with oils, vinegars, sauces, dressings, preserves, pastes, herbs and spices not only look appealing but are fundamental to the success of so many dishes. A spoonful of spice paste or a splash of chilli oil, for instance, can transform a dish into something special. The prerequisites for a store cupboard are that it should be cool and dark, ensuring that its contents remain in the best condition.

My store cupboard houses a range of vinegars. Balsamic, wine, rice wine, cider and malt vinegar can all be used on their own or as part of a preserve. Flavoured vinegars or fresh relishes benefit from good-quality wine vinegar or cider vinegar, while you can get away with a more economical and robust malt vinegar in strongly flavoured chutneys and pickles. Use a vinegar that is at least 5 per cent acid (this is normally mentioned on the label), as home-made preserves should have a low pH or a high acidity if they are to last for a decent length of time.

You should also have a selection of oils to hand. There's the (essential) extra virgin olive oil, plus a lighter one for cooking, a toasted sesame oil for Asian dishes, a good-quality rapeseed or grapeseed oil and a small bottle of truffle oil, a splash of which transforms many a meal. I also like to make my own flavoured oils using herbs, chillies, spices and citrus zest. I've found that herbs grown organically have the best flavour and keeping qualities and it's also best to use unwaxed citrus fruit. Flavoured oils are best made in small quantities as they deteriorate with time and I would advise storing them in the fridge and using within a few weeks. If flavoured oils become too warm, there is a risk they will become rancid and there is also a low, but possible, risk of spoilage caused by moulds and the bacterium *Clostridium botulinum* (botulism). This is because you are preserving an ingredient in a low-acid environment and without heating it to boiling point first, which kills off many unwanted bacteria. You have to be particularly careful when flavouring oils with fresh garlic or chilli. The former is best used within a few days of making, although the oil will keep for up to a month if the garlic is roasted or blanched first. Similarly, chillies should be roasted or blanched, or you could use dried chillies. Dried herbs and spices are a good and possible safer alternative to fresh and will produce flavoured oils with a longer shelf life but not quite such a fresh flavour.

FRUIT & VEGETABLES

Fruit can be bottled whole in sugar syrup or alcohol, it can be cooked down to make jam or, like vegetables, it can be made into a chutney or pickle to spice up cold meat, cheese, pies or curries. Preserving is a perfect method of using up a glut of a particular type of fruit (or vegetable), but bear in mind that the best-quality fresh produce will produce the best-quality preserve. So damaged, bruised, old and soft specimens are best avoided.

Having said this, when making jam it's preferable to use fruit that is slightly under-ripe as it will have a higher acidity level as well as more pectin, both of which will help the jam to set. It's not necessary to make a large quantity, in fact, even a regular-sized punnet of strawberries is sufficient to make a jar of jam in little more than 10 minutes.

If you intend to keep a sweet preserve for any length of time, you need to use a sufficient amount of sugar and cook the preserve at a high temperature (85°C/180°F). Sweet preserves should keep for up to two years if they are stored in a cool, dark place, but they should be kept in the fridge once opened and eaten within a few months.

Fruit and vegetable chutneys not only make great accompaniments to meals, but a spoonful can also add extra oomph to stews, sauces and curries. On top of fruit and vegetables, a chutney needs a combination of sugar, vinegar and salt, which, if used in the right proportions, will ensure the chutney has a decent shelf life and allow the flavours to mature. Spices add flavour and act as a preservative: coriander seeds, cumin, star anise, nutmeg, cardamom, juniper, dried chilli and mustard seeds all work well.

The exact difference between a chutney and a pickle is not crystal clear. In my interpretation, a chutney is a mixture of chopped fruit and vegetables simmered down until reduced and thickened, whereas a pickle contains firmer, crispier, larger pieces (or whole) fresh produce such as onions, shallots, beetroots, cauliflowers, red cabbages, pears and apples – not forgetting walnuts and eggs! The fresh produce is either cooked or left raw.

Vegetables with a high water content, such as cucumbers, marrows and courgettes, will need brining or dry-salting before pickling to remove excess water. Then there's a relish, which tends to be made of finely chopped or grated fresh produce, rather like a chutney, but is fresher and therefore best eaten on the day of making. There are anomalies, of course, but there's no denying that many dishes would be duller without the addition of these preserves.

HOW TO STERILIZE JARS

There is nothing more satisfying and rewarding than making your own preserved foods. With all types of preserving, paying careful attention to hygiene and safety is paramount, but it's all pretty straightforward if you stick to the guidelines here.

Glass jars with either a screw-top or Kilner fixing are suitable for most preserves. They don't have to be brand new, but it's essential they are sterilized before use. Firstly, remove any labels if reusing jars. Wash both new and reused jars well in hot soapy water, then rinse them and put upside down, without their lids, on a baking tray in a cold oven. Turn the heat to 180°C/350°F/Gas 4 and, once the oven has reached this temperature, leave the jars in the oven for 20 minutes to ensure they are completely sterilized. Most preserves will still be hot when potted so it makes sense to keep the jars in the oven until needed, but you can reduce the heat slightly. As an alternative to sterilizing jars in the oven, they can be boiled in a pan of water for 10 minutes, then dried upside down in the oven, as described above.

For hygiene reasons, especially if you want a full seal, always use new lids (you can buy packs of them in various sizes from kitchen shops and online) and sterilize them by boiling in a pan of water for 10 minutes. Make sure they are dry before use to avoid condensation forming. An alternative method of sterilizing lids is to fill the hot jars with the hot preserve, then screw on the new lids and turn the jars upside down for 1 minute – when you do this, make sure you are wearing gloves or cover the jar with a kitchen towel in order to avoid burning yourself. This effectively sterilizes the insides of the lids and means that you don't need to use wax paper or film discs to cover the preserve before putting the lids on.

FILLING, POTTING & STORING

It's best to fill a hot jar with a hot preserve. If you pot at around 80°C/170°F, this will ensure a longer shelf life. If the jar is not hot it is advisable to warm it, as pouring boiling hot preserve into a cold jar can cause the jar to shatter. In my experience this is rare and generally only happens if there is a fault in the glass which may not be visible, so it is best to be cautious.

1   When filling a jar, fill it to within 1cm/½in of the rim and, before sealing, tap the jar on a hard surface or run a sterilized spoon through the contents of the jar to release any trapped air pockets.
2   Seal the jar with a new, sterilized lid immediately after filling to prevent contamination. (You may need to tighten the lids again when the jars have cooled.)
3   Wipe the jars clean and label them, making a note of the contents and the date. You may think you'll remember these details but they're easily forgotten.

If potting an uncooked preserve, you can pasteurize it so it lasts longer. This can be done in two ways: the first is to put the filled jars on a rack in a large saucepan, making sure that they do not touch each other. Pour in enough water to come halfway up the sides of the jars. Bring the water to the boil, then turn the heat down slightly and simmer with a lid on for 1 hour. The second way is to pasteurize the filled jars in a vegetable steamer for 1 hour. Whichever method you use, always keep an eye on the water level and top up with more water when needed. Don't forget that acidity and sugar concentration will both play a part in the shelf life of the finished product.

Store jarred or bottled preserves in a cool, dark place and then in the fridge after opening. All chutneys, pickles, mustards, jams and marmalades benefit from a period of maturation to allow the flavour to develop and mellow. They may darken in colour, too, during this time, but this should not be a cause for alarm if they are made and packed using the guidelines given here.

EQUIPMENT

A **kitchen thermometer** is essential when making preserves. It helps you gauge the correct setting point when making jams and marmalades, and also ensures your preserve reaches the necessary temperature to destroy any unwanted bugs.

Bacteria is most active between 10°C/50°F and 50°C/120°F, and while chilling or freezing restrains activity, these processes don't kill them. However, boiling at 85°C/180°F will kill most yeasts and moulds, but not spore-forming bacteria which can be controlled in most cases by acidity and sugar concentration. If you want to get serious about the process of preserving, a **digital pH meter** is also useful. This will allow you to check your preserve's acidity, which can help to get a better set in jams and, with a bit of knowledge, to ascertain its potential shelf life.

One of the most useful pieces of equipment in my kitchen is a **stick blender** as it is a convenient and simple way of puréeing fruit and vegetables, and making mayonnaise, batter mixes, breadcrumbs and dressings. A **preserving pan** is great if you have one as it's designed for purpose with a thick, heavy base so you can keep your preserve at a rolling boil without it sticking. They also have graduated sides for easy measuring and to ensure any liquid evaporates quickly, as well as a pouring spout to make filling easier. But a preserving pan is not essential; if you don't have one, opt for a wide, deep stainless steel or enamel saucepan, and avoid aluminium as it will taint the flavour of your preserve. A **jam funnel** can be useful for filling jars without spills, but do make sure that it is sterilized first.

If your preserve contains a high percentage of vinegar then you will need to use **vinegar-proof lids**; these are the ones that have white plastic on the underside. Alternatively, a **Kilner jar** with a rubber seal is fine. As mentioned earlier, it's not essential to use new jars, but I would always recommend using new lids.

RECIPES TO TREASURE

Today, no deli would be worth its weight in gold without an inspirational and mouth-watering selection of delicious goodies, from a cave-ripened Roquefort and layered seafood terrine to a hot-water crust pork pie and exquisite fruit-packed preserve. I hope that my collection of recipes in this book will be equally inspiring, and they prove to be as much a feast for the eyes as for the taste buds.

1. Meat & Poultry

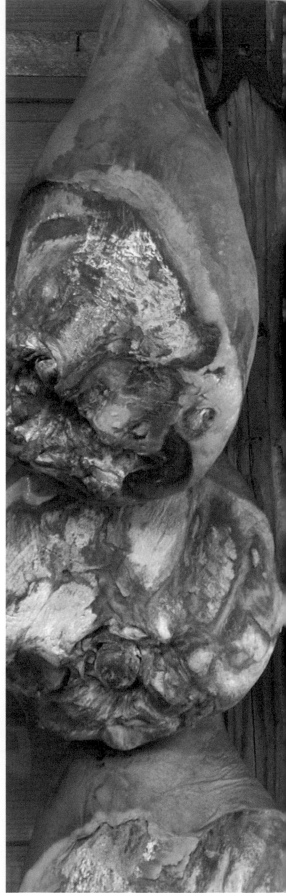

Duck Rillettes

Making rillettes is a good way of preserving meat. The duck is slow-roasted first to render the fat, which in turn can be used for potting, and to give the meat a great depth of flavour. Depending on how fatty your duck legs are, you may not be able to use them to create extra fat for potting, in which case you can buy additional duck or goose fat. The rillettes will keep for up to 2 weeks in the fridge.

**SERVES 6 PREPARATION TIME: 30 MINUTES, PLUS COOLING AND INFUSING
COOKING TIME: 2 HOURS 10 MINUTES**

2 tsp sea salt, plus extra to taste
¼ tsp freshly ground black pepper, plus extra to taste
½ tsp Chinese five-spice powder or mixed spice
4 good-sized, fatty duck legs
100ml/3½ fl oz/generous ⅓ cup white wine
2 star anise
2 garlic cloves, cut into slices
about 100ml/3½ fl oz/generous ⅓ cup duck or goose fat (as needed)
toast or crackers and a green salad, to serve

Preheat the oven to 150°C/300°F/Gas 2. Mix together the salt, pepper and Chinese five-spice powder. Rub the spice mixture all over the flesh side of the duck legs.

Put the duck legs skin-side up in a tight-fitting roasting tin. Spoon any spices left over the duck. Pour 2 tablespoons water into the tin, cover tightly with foil so the duck cooks in its own fat and roast for 2 hours until the meat is almost falling off the bone but is still moist. Remove from the oven and leave to cool completely, still covered with foil.

Remove the duck from the roasting tin and scrape off any cooking fat into a small pan. Discard the skin and remove all the duck meat into a bowl. Shred the meat into rough strips using your hands or two forks. Discard the bones.

Put the wine, star anise and garlic in a saucepan and bring to the boil. Let the wine bubble away until reduced by three-quarters, then add the fat from the duck and any juices left in the tin. You need to have sufficient fat to cover the duck to preserve it. If you don't have enough fat from the roasted duck at this point, add extra duck or goose fat. Return the mixture to the boil, then remove from the heat, season with salt and plenty of pepper and leave for 30 minutes so that the flavours infuse.

Remove the garlic and star anise with a slotted spoon, then pour the mixture over the shredded duck. Pack the duck into six large ramekins or a terrine dish. Leave to cool, then chill, covered, until ready to serve. Serve with toast or crackers and a green leaf salad, or see the Chinese Pancakes with Crispy Duck Rillettes on page 17.

CHINESE PANCAKES WITH CRISPY
DUCK RILLETTES

In this recipe the Duck Rillettes (see page 16) are used to make an excellent alternative to the traditional Chinese Peking duck, but unlike this classic Beijing dish, you use just the meat rather than a combination of meat and skin. Purists will not be disappointed, however, as the crispy duck is served with all the usual accoutrements.

SERVES 4   PREPARATION TIME: 15 MINUTES   COOKING TIME: 15 MINUTES

1 recipe quantity Duck Rillettes
  (see page 16)
½ cucumber, sliced lengthways,
  deseeded and cut into thin strips

4 spring onions, shredded
4 tbsp hoisin sauce or Chinese Plum
  Sauce (see page 121)
16 Chinese pancakes

Scrape off as much fat as possible from the duck rillettes. Heat a wok over a high heat. Add half the duck, turn the heat down slightly and stir-fry for 5 minutes until crisp. Remove the duck from the wok using a slotted spoon, drain on kitchen paper and keep warm until ready to serve. Carefully pour away or spoon off any excess fat from the wok. Repeat with the remaining duck.

Put the cucumber, spring onions and hoisin sauce in three separate dishes until ready to serve.

Steam the pancakes in two batches for a few minutes until warmed through. Wrap the pancakes in foil to keep them warm while you cook the second batch.

To serve, allow everyone to help themselves, rolling up the duck, cucumber and spring onion-filled pancakes and dipping them in the hoisin sauce before eating.

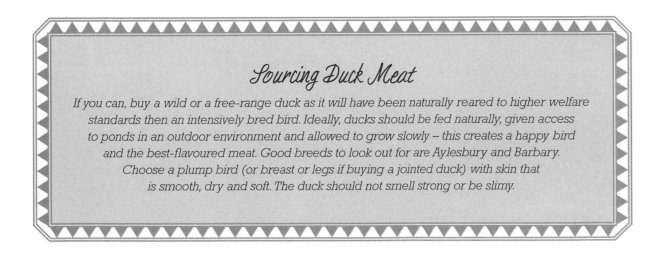

Sourcing Duck Meat

If you can, buy a wild or a free-range duck as it will have been naturally reared to higher welfare standards then an intensively bred bird. Ideally, ducks should be fed naturally, given access to ponds in an outdoor environment and allowed to grow slowly – this creates a happy bird and the best-flavoured meat. Good breeds to look out for are Aylesbury and Barbary. Choose a plump bird (or breast or legs if buying a jointed duck) with skin that is smooth, dry and soft. The duck should not smell strong or be slimy.

GAME, CHICKEN & APRICOT PIE

This raised pie has a hot-water pastry crust and, contrary to the normal rules of pastry-making when everything should be kept as cool as possible, this pastry is used when still warm. The pastry is made by melting fat in water and milk, and bringing it to the boil before beating in the flour. This makes a substantial dough, perfect for encasing pork, ham and game pies without collapsing. I like to serve this pie simply with new potatoes and a green salad, but it also makes a great centrepiece at a picnic, cut into decent-sized slices and served with a generous spoonful of chutney.

**SERVES 8–10 PREPARATION TIME: 30 MINUTES, PLUS COOLING
COOKING TIME: 2 HOURS 20 MINUTES**

PASTRY:
100ml/3½ fl oz/generous ⅓ cup milk
175g/6oz lard, plus extra for greasing
2 eggs
525g/1lb 2½ oz/scant 4¼ cups plain flour,
   plus extra for dusting
1 tsp salt

FILLING:
40g/1½ oz butter
4 shallots, finely chopped
2 garlic cloves, finely chopped

575g/1lb 4½ oz cubed pork shoulder
150g/5½ oz streaky bacon, finely chopped
1 tsp dried thyme
1 tbsp chopped sage leaves
1–2 tsp ground allspice
1 tsp juniper berries, crushed
2 tbsp brandy
225g/8oz skinless, boneless pheasant, sliced
85g/3oz dried apricots, halved crossways
225g/8oz skinless, boneless chicken
   thighs, sliced
sea salt and freshly ground black pepper

To make the filling, heat the butter in a large frying pan over a medium heat and fry the shallots and garlic for 5 minutes until softened. Transfer to a bowl and leave to cool.

Mince the pork shoulder in a food processor and transfer to a large bowl with the bacon, thyme, sage allspice, juniper berries, brandy and cooled shallots and garlic. Season with salt and pepper and stir until combined. (Check the seasoning by frying a little nugget of the mixture, adding more salt and pepper to taste.) Leave to one side.

Preheat the oven to 200°C/400°F/Gas 6. Grease a 20cm/8in springform tin with lard and line the base and sides with baking paper. Put 100ml/3½fl oz generous ⅓ cup water in a saucepan with the milk and lard and bring to the boil, stirring until combined.

Meanwhile, lightly beat 1 of the eggs. Mix together the flour and salt in a mixing bowl, make a central well and pour in the egg and the hot lard mixture. Beat with a wooden spoon until you have a smooth dough.

Turn out the dough onto a lightly floured work surface and, when cool enough to handle, knead briefly. Cut off a third of the pastry and wrap in cling film to keep it warm. Roll out the remaining warm pastry on a lightly floured work surface and use to line the base and sides of the tin. It has a tendency to pull itself down, but persevere and patch up any holes or cracks.

CONTINUED ON PAGE **20**

Spoon half of the mince mixture into the pastry-lined tin. Top with a layer of pheasant, then add the apricots and chicken. Top with the remaining mince mixture, pressing it down to make an even layer.

Lightly beat the remaining egg. Roll out the reserved pastry into a circle on a lightly floured work surface. Brush the top of the pastry sides with the egg and top with the pastry. Trim the pastry lid and pinch the edges together to seal securely. Cut a 1cm/½in hole in the centre and brush the top with egg. Cut shapes from the pastry offcuts to decorate and brush them with more egg.

Bake for 20 minutes, then reduce the oven temperature to 170°C/325°F/Gas 3. Cover the top with foil to prevent it browning too much and bake for a further 1¾ hours until golden brown.

Remove the pie from the oven and remove the sides of the tin. Brush the sides with more egg and bake for another 10 minutes until golden. Insert a skewer into the top of the pie and if the juices run clear, the pie is cooked. Leave to cool. It will keep in the fridge for up to 5 days.

COOK'S TIPS
• If the pastry is too fragile when you first roll it out, simply re-form it into a ball, leave for a moment and then re-roll again. Don't let it become cold, though, as it will be difficult to use, becoming stiff and crumbly.
• Some recommend using both butter and lard to make hot-water pastry for a slightly richer flavour, so you could try replacing 50g/1¾oz of the lard with the same quantity of butter, if preferred.

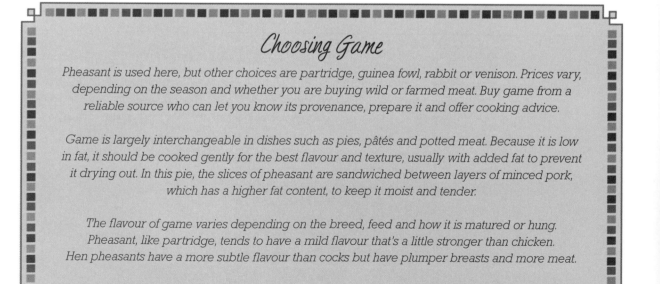

Choosing Game

Pheasant is used here, but other choices are partridge, guinea fowl, rabbit or venison. Prices vary, depending on the season and whether you are buying wild or farmed meat. Buy game from a reliable source who can let you know its provenance, prepare it and offer cooking advice.

Game is largely interchangeable in dishes such as pies, pâtés and potted meat. Because it is low in fat, it should be cooked gently for the best flavour and texture, usually with added fat to prevent it drying out. In this pie, the slices of pheasant are sandwiched between layers of minced pork, which has a higher fat content, to keep it moist and tender.

The flavour of game varies depending on the breed, feed and how it is matured or hung. Pheasant, like partridge, tends to have a mild flavour that's a little stronger than chicken. Hen pheasants have a more subtle flavour than cocks but have plumper breasts and more meat.

PASTRAMI WITH SWEET CUCUMBER RELISH ON RYE

An adaptation of the New York deli classic, this pastrami on rye comes with a fresh cucumber relish instead of the usual gherkins. Pastrami is cured, dried beef and is best served in thin slices.

SERVES 4   PREPARATION TIME: 20 MINUTES, PLUS SALTING   COOKING TIME: 3 MINUTES

2 tbsp mayonnaise
1 tsp English mustard
8 slices of light rye bread
16 slices of pastrami

SWEET CUCUMBER RELISH:
1 small cucumber, ends trimmed
3 tbsp good-quality white wine vinegar
　or rice wine vinegar
3 tbsp caster sugar
1 tbsp chopped dill
sea salt

To make the sweet cucumber relish, cut the cucumber into long, thin slices using a vegetable peeler or mandolin. Put the slices in a colander and cover with salt. Leave for 20 minutes to drain, then rinse off the salt and pat the cucumber dry.

Meanwhile, mix together the mayonnaise and English mustard and leave to one side.

Mix together the vinegar and sugar in a bowl large enough to hold the cucumber until the sugar dissolves. Add the cucumber and dill and turn in the vinegar mixture until combined.

Preheat the grill to high and lightly toast both sides of the rye bread. Spread each slice of toast with a little of the mustard mayonnaise, then top with 2 slices of pastrami. Drain the cucumber and lay it in folds on top of the pastrami before serving.

Home-Cured Bacon

For the most superior bacon, use a pork belly with distinct layers of fat and meat, preferably from a Saddleback, Gloucester Old Spot or Middle White pig. If you can't find smoked salt, increase the coarse sea salt. Cut the bacon thickly as lardons or thinly and serve as part of a fry-up.

MAKES ABOUT 600G/1LB 5OZ   PREPARATION TIME: ABOUT 5 DAYS

600g/1lb 5oz boneless pork belly
60g/2¼ oz coarse sea salt
1 tbsp smoked salt
1 tbsp clear honey
1 tbsp demerara sugar

Pat dry the pork belly all over and remove the rind, if you like. Mix together both types of salt, the honey and sugar in a non-metallic bowl. Rub the mixture over both sides of the pork until completely covered. Put the pork in a thick ziplock freezer bag, expel as much air as possible, then seal. Put the bag on a plate and prop up one end so any liquid released from the pork runs away to the side.

Put the bag in a dish in the fridge for 3 days. Each day, pour off any liquid, reseal and return to the fridge. After 3 days, rinse the salt off the pork then pat it dry. (To test the taste, cut a small piece off and pan-fry it; if the bacon is too salty for your taste, soak it for 1 hour in water, then pat dry again.)

Put a rack inside a deep plastic, glass or ceramic dish. Put the pork on top and leave it in a cool, well-ventilated place for 2 days, covered with a piece of clean muslin. Remove the bacon from the dish, wrap in greaseproof paper and store in the fridge until ready to eat. A 5-day cure gives a lightly salted bacon, which will keep for up to 1 month, or it can be frozen for up to 3 months.

BACON, NECTARINE & GINGER SALAD

The combination of crisp, salty bacon and sweet, juicy nectarine with the heat from the stem ginger is a real winner in this salad. It is dressed simply in lemon juice and extra virgin olive oil, which enhance the flavours of the main ingredients.

SERVES 4   PREPARATION TIME: 10 MINUTES   COOKING TIME: 7 MINUTES

8 thin Home-Cured Bacon rashers
  (see page 22)
2 balls of stem ginger, diced, plus 2 tbsp
  syrup from the jar
100g/3½ oz soft leaf salad
100g/3½ oz pea shoots
2 ripe nectarines, cut in half, stoned and
  sliced lengthways

DRESSING:
4 tbsp extra virgin olive oil, preferably
  a fruit-flavoured one
2 tbsp lemon juice
sea salt and freshly ground black pepper

Preheat the grill to high and line the grill pan with foil. Grill the bacon for 5 minutes, turning once. Brush one side with the ginger syrup and grill for another 1 minute, then turn the bacon over and repeat until crisp and golden. Leave to cool slightly and break into large bite-sized pieces.

Meanwhile, mix together all the ingredients for the dressing and season with salt and pepper.

Put the salad leaves and pea shoots on a serving plate or bowl and top with the nectarines and stem ginger. Spoon as much of the dressing over as needed, then toss gently until lightly coated. Scatter the bacon pieces over the top and serve straight away.

QUAIL SCOTCH EGGS

These Scotch eggs are just the perfect size and are so satisfying to make – and they are great for a summer party, picnic or snack. Use good-quality sausage meat or squeeze the filling out of ready-made thick pork sausages – a Cumberland sausage is a good one to use. If you do use a herby sausage meat, then it's best to leave out the sage.

MAKES 12   PREPARATION TIME: 30 MINUTES   COOKING TIME: 20 MINUTES

12 quail's eggs
1 tsp fennel seeds
500g/1lb 2oz good-quality sausage meat
1 tbsp chopped sage leaves
2 eggs

100g/3½ oz/1¼ cups fresh breadcrumbs
100g/3½ oz/heaped ¾ cup plain flour
sunflower oil, for deep-frying
sea salt and freshly ground black pepper

Put the quail's eggs in a pan, cover with just-boiled water and return to a gentle boil for 2½ minutes. Drain the eggs, cool under cold running water and peel.

Meanwhile, toast the fennel seeds in a dry frying pan over a medium heat for 1–2 minutes until they smell aromatic. Mix together the sausage meat, fennel seeds and sage until combined. Season with salt and pepper.

Beat the eggs in a shallow bowl. Tip the breadcrumbs and flour into two separate shallow bowls and season the latter with salt and pepper.

Take a heaped tablespoon of the sausage meat in the palm of your hand and flatten it out slightly into a round. Lightly dust a quail's egg in the flour, then put it in the centre of the sausage meat. Wrap the sausage meat around the egg and press together the edges to make a round about the size of a golf ball. Dust the Scotch egg in the flour and pat away any excess, then dip into the egg and roll in the breadcrumbs. Put it on a plate and repeat to make 12 Scotch eggs in total.

Heat enough oil in a deep pan to deep-fry the Scotch eggs. It is hot enough when a small piece of bread turns golden and crisp in 30 seconds. Deep-fry 4 Scotch eggs at a time for 3–4 minutes, turning them occasionally until golden and crisp all over. Drain on kitchen paper and repeat to cook all the Scotch eggs. Leave to cool before serving.

HAM HOCK, ROASTED BEETROOT & PORCINI LENTILS

This rustic and wholesome dish makes the perfect meal on a cold winter's night and is just the thing if you're looking for something warming and satisfying. While this recipe uses ready-cooked ham hock, it is an inexpensive cut to buy and straightforward to cook, requiring long and slow braising or roasting. It's delicious with lentils, as here, or with mash, cabbage or peas, as well as in soups, stews and roasts.

SERVES 4   PREPARATION TIME: 15 MINUTES   COOKING TIME: 45 MINUTES

3 uncooked beetroots, peeled and each cut into 8 wedges
3 tbsp olive oil
235g/8½ oz/heaped 1¼ cups green lentils
2 good-quality porcini or chicken stock cubes
1 large onion
2 garlic cloves, chopped
1 red pepper, halved lengthways, deseeded and roughly chopped

150g/5½ oz cherry tomatoes, halved
2 tsp dried thyme
2 tsp Dijon mustard
juice of 1 lemon
1 handful of flat-leaf parsley leaves, roughly chopped
125g/4½ oz cooked and shredded smoked ham hock
sea salt and freshly ground black pepper

Preheat the oven to 190°C/375°F/Gas 5. Put the beetroot in a roasting tin and brush 1 tablespoon of the olive oil over. Season with salt and pepper and bake for 40–45 minutes, turning once, until tender and slightly caramelized.

Meanwhile, put the lentils in a pan and pour enough water over to cover them by about 2cm/¾in. Bring to the boil, then crumble in the stock cubes and stir until combined. Turn the heat down and simmer, partially covered, for 25 minutes or until tender; then drain.

Heat the remaining oil in a large frying pan over a medium heat and fry the onion for 8 minutes until softened. Add the garlic, red pepper and tomatoes and fry for 3 minutes until softened, then stir in the thyme, mustard and lemon juice.

Fold in the parsley, ham and lentils, taking care not to break up the lentils, and heat through. Season with pepper before serving with the roasted beetroot.

COUNTRY-STYLE PÂTÉ

This rustic French pâté is made from economical cuts of pork and flavoured with a healthy quantity of garlic, juniper berries, brandy and thyme.

**MAKES 900G/2LB   PREPARATION TIME: 30 MINUTES, PLUS CHILLING
COOKING TIME: 1 HOUR 35 MINUTES**

25g/1oz butter
425g/15oz pork livers, trimmed of sinew and sliced into strips
325g/11½ oz pork shoulder, roughly chopped
325g/11½ oz pork belly, rind cut off and roughly chopped
3 tsp sea salt

3 garlic cloves, crushed
10 black peppercorns
10 juniper berries
1 tsp dried thyme
½ tsp ground mace
3 tbsp brandy
10–12 thin streaky bacon rashers

Melt the butter in a large frying pan and cook the livers in two batches over a medium heat for 1½ minutes on each side or until just coloured on the outside.

Mince the pork shoulder, belly and livers in a food processor. Transfer the pork mixture to a bowl. Grind the sea salt with the garlic, peppercorns and juniper berries to a coarse paste, then stir it into the pork mixture with the thyme, mace and brandy. Cover and chill for 1 hour to allow the flavours to develop.

Preheat the oven to 150°C/300°F/Gas 2. Put the bacon between two sheets of cling film and roll out to stretch it lengthways. Line a 900g/2lb terrine dish or loaf tin with the bacon, reserving 2–3 rashers, letting the bacon hang over the top of the tin.

Spoon the pâté mixture into the dish and level the top, then fold the bacon over and lay the remaining rashers lengthways along the pâté until it is covered.

Put the pâté in a roasting tin and pour in enough just-boiled water to come halfway up the sides of the tin. Bake for 1½ hours, covering the pâté after 1 hour with foil to prevent it browning too much, or until the pâté shrinks from the tin sides and the juices run clear when a skewer is inserted into the centre.

Remove the pâté from the roasting tin and leave it to cool in the terrine dish – the juices surrounding the pâté will set into a jelly when cool. The pâté will keep for up to 1 week stored in the fridge.

Smoked Chicken

Smoking is one of the oldest methods of preserving or adding flavour and this preparation technique gives a new dimension to regular cuts of meat, poultry and fish. This recipe is for hot-smoked chicken which, rather than preserving the meat, infuses it with a gentle smokiness as well as cooking it. Special equipment is not needed; a large wok with a lid does the job perfectly. The smoked chicken makes a great addition to a salad with a creamy dressing and new potatoes. Alternatively, add it to the paella on page 29.

SERVES 4   PREPARATION TIME: 15 MINUTES, PLUS MARINATING
COOKING TIME: 18 MINUTES

1 heaped tsp smoked paprika
2 tsp dried oregano
1 tbsp soft light brown sugar
½ tsp sea salt
4 tsp olive oil
4 skinless, boneless chicken breasts, about 175g/6oz each

SMOKING MIXTURE:
4 large handfuls of white rice
2 handfuls of loose black tea leaves
4 tbsp demerara sugar
2 long rosemary sprigs

Mix together the smoked paprika, oregano, sugar, salt and olive oil.

Put the chicken between two sheets of cling film and flatten with a meat mallet or rolling pin until about 2cm/¾in thick. This will ensure the chicken cooks evenly and allows the smoke to penetrate the meat. Spread the paprika mixture over the chicken and marinate, covered, for at least 1 hour in the fridge.

To prepare the smoker, line the base and lid of a wok with foil. Put the wok on a wok stand, if you have one, to keep it stable. Mix together the white rice, black tea and sugar in the base of the wok and lay the rosemary on top. Lightly grease a wire rack and put it over the top of the smoking mixture, making sure it does not touch.

Put the chicken on the rack and cover with the foil-lined lid. Heat the wok over a medium heat until you start to see little wisps of smoke escaping around the lid. Carefully patch up any leaks with foil, turn the heat down to medium-low and make sure the kitchen is well ventilated.

Smoke the chicken for about 18 minutes until it is cooked through; there should be no trace of pinkness when the breasts are pierced with a skewer.

PAELLA WITH **SMOKED CHICKEN** & PRAWNS

The smoked chicken adds depth of flavour to this classic Spanish rice dish, and it's a glorious reminder of sunny summer holidays.

SERVES 4   PREPARATION TIME: 20 MINUTES, PLUS RESTING   COOKING TIME: 45 MINUTES

1 large pinch of saffron threads
2 tbsp olive oil
85g/3oz cooking chorizo, roughly chopped
1 large onion, finely chopped
1 red pepper, deseeded and chopped
2 large garlic cloves, chopped
375g/13oz/scant 1¾ cups bomba or Calasparra paella rice
185ml/6fl oz/¾ cup dry white wine

1.1l/38fl oz/4½ cups good-quality hot chicken stock, plus extra if needed
1 heaped tsp smoked hot paprika
¾ recipe quantity Smoked Chicken (see page 28), cut into bite-sized pieces
3 handfuls of frozen petit pois
8 jumbo raw prawns in the shell
12 vine-ripened cherry tomatoes, halved
sea salt and freshly ground black pepper
lemon wedges, to serve

Cover the saffron threads with a little hot water and leave to one side to infuse. Heat the olive oil in a paella dish or a wide, deep frying pan with a lid. Add the chorizo and fry for a few minutes until almost crisp, then, using a slotted spoon, remove from the pan and leave to one side.

Add the onion to the pan and cook for 5 minutes until softened, then add the red pepper and garlic and cook for another 2 minutes. Add the rice and stir until all the grains are coated and glossy.

Add the wine and when it is bubbling and has reduced a little, pour in the stock and the saffron threads and soaking liquid and stir in the paprika. Cook over a medium-low heat for 15 minutes, without stirring but shaking the pan occasionally.

Stir in the chorizo, chicken, peas, prawns and tomatoes, season with salt and pepper and cook for another 10–15 minutes until the rice is tender but still retains its shape and everything is cooked through; add a little extra stock if the paella looks too dry. Cover the pan with a baking sheet and leave the paella to rest for 5 minutes off the heat. Serve with lemon wedges for squeezing over.

Bomba Rice

Bomba is considered the king of paella rices. Grown around Valencia in Spain, this short-grain rice has a soft, yielding texture when cooked, yet keeps its shape. Its name comes from the way each grain expands widthways during cooking to form "little bombs". One of the key features of this ancient strain of rice is its absorbency, and so it takes on all the flavours of the stock and other ingredients in the paella.

Confit of Duck

Originally a confit was made to preserve foods such as meat, poultry, fish or vegetables for the long winter months when there was little fresh food. It is an ancient way of preserving foods and is particularly popular in French cuisine. Confit of Duck makes a delicious foundation for many meals, including the traditional Cassoulet (see page 33). You can also scrape the fat from the duck and roast the legs in a hot oven (200°C/400°F/Gas 6) for 15 minutes until the skin crisps up. Serve with a green salad, or mashed potatoes and red cabbage, or with Puy lentils.

SERVES 4   PREPARATION TIME: 10 MINUTES, PLUS OVERNIGHT SALTING AND 1 WEEK MATURING   COOKING TIME: 1 HOUR 40 MINUTES

4 good-sized fatty duck legs
4 tsp rock salt
1 tbsp black peppercorns
3 garlic cloves, sliced
2 bay leaves, torn into pieces
4 thyme sprigs

FOR POTTING:
about 670ml/23fl oz/2⅔ cups duck or goose fat
2 bay leaves
6 garlic cloves, peeled
a few thyme sprigs

Put the duck legs in a non-metallic dish and sprinkle the salt, peppercorns, garlic, bay leaves and thyme over the flesh side of each leg. Cover the dish with cling film and leave in the fridge overnight.

Preheat the oven to 150°C/300°F/ Gas 2. Brush the salt, pepper and other flavourings off the duck, rinse the legs under cold running water and pat dry with kitchen paper.

Cut away any loose bits of skin and put these in a large flameproof casserole along with the duck legs, skin-side down; you ideally want them to be in a single layer. Cook the duck legs over a gentle heat until the fat starts to run, then turn the heat up slightly and cook for a few minutes to colour the skin.

Turn the duck over and add the duck or goose fat. Add the bay leaves, garlic and thyme. Heat until the fat has melted and covers the duck. Cover with a lid and transfer the casserole to the oven for 1½ hours until the duck is very tender.

Leave the duck to cool slightly in the casserole, then transfer to a sterilized earthenware crock or large jar. Pour the fat over the duck so that it is completely submerged, leaving any duck juices in the bottom of the casserole behind. Leave to cool and store in the fridge, leaving the confit for 1 week before eating to allow the flavours to mature. Store for up to 3 months in the fridge.

CASSOULET WITH **CONFIT OF DUCK**

This classic French slow-cooked stew typically contains a hearty mixture of haricot beans, confit of duck, bacon and sausages, and mutton is often included too. Rich, warming and filling, it makes a great wintery dish served with steamed kale and slices of crusty French bread.

**SERVES 4   PREPARATION TIME: 20 MINUTES, PLUS OVERNIGHT SOAKING
COOKING TIME: 2¾ HOURS**

200g/7oz/1 cup dried haricot beans
½ recipe quantity Confit of Duck
   (see page 32)
175g/6oz lardons
350g/12oz pork shoulder, cut into large
   bite-sized pieces trimmed of fat
1 large onion, chopped
2 carrots, chopped
1 celery stick, sliced
2 bay leaves
2 tsp dried thyme
250ml/9fl oz/1 cup dry cider or white wine

200g/7oz chopped tomatoes
1 good-quality chicken stock cube
200g/7oz smoked sausage, sliced
freshly ground black pepper
steamed kale and French bread, to serve

TOPPING:
1 tbsp olive oil
125g/4½ oz/1½ cups fresh breadcrumbs
1 large garlic clove, crushed
2 tbsp chopped parsley leaves

Put the beans in a large bowl and pour enough cold water over to cover. Leave to soak, covered, overnight. The next day, drain and rinse the beans under cold running water. Put them in a large pan and cover with plenty of cold water. Bring to the boil, then allow to bubble away for 15 minutes. Drain and leave to one side.

Meanwhile, heat a large flameproof casserole. Scrape off the fat surrounding the duck and sear the duck in the hot casserole, skin-side down, for a few minutes until brown and crisp. Leave to drain on kitchen paper.

Pour off all but 1 tablespoon of the fat in the casserole and add the lardons. Fry, stirring occasionally, for 5 minutes or until starting to crisp. Leave to drain on kitchen paper. Repeat with the pork shoulder.

Preheat the oven to 160°C/315°F/Gas 2–3. Add the onion, carrots and celery to the casserole and cook for 5 minutes until softened, then return the lardons, duck and pork shoulder. Add the half-cooked haricot beans, bay leaves, thyme, cider, 500ml/17fl oz/2 cups water and chopped tomatoes. Bring to the boil, then turn the heat down and stir in the stock cube and smoked sausage.

Cover with a lid and transfer the casserole to the oven and cook for 1 hour. Remove the lid and cook for another 1 hour until the sauce has reduced and thickened and the beans are tender. Season with pepper (you are unlikely to need salt).

Meanwhile, make the topping. Heat the oil in a frying pan over a medium heat and fry the breadcrumbs for 4 minutes until starting to colour. Add the garlic and cook for another 2–3 minutes until the crumbs are crisp and golden. Remove from the heat and stir in the parsley. Sprinkle the cassoulet with the crispy breadcrumbs and serve with kale and French bread.

MERGUEZ SAUSAGES WITH SMOKED PAPRIKA BEANS

These thin, dark sausages originate in North Africa and are made from lamb or mutton (sometimes beef) and are heavily spiced, often with harissa. This dish is a sort of posh beans on toast and makes a simple weekday meal. If you can't find a jar of butter bean gigantes, use canned beans instead.

SERVES 4   PREPARATION TIME: 15 MINUTES   COOKING TIME: 17 MINUTES

10 merguez sausages
3 tbsp olive oil, plus extra for brushing
1 red pepper, deseeded and roughly chopped
4 garlic cloves, finely chopped
3 large vine-ripened tomatoes, quartered, deseeded and chopped
1 tbsp thyme leaves
1 tsp smoked hot paprika

800g/1lb 12oz jarred butter bean gigantes or tinned butter beans, drained and rinsed
100g/3½ oz baby spinach leaves
1 tsp Dijon mustard
juice of 1 lemon
4 large, thick slices of country-style bread
sea salt and freshly ground black pepper
small handful of coriander leaves, for sprinkling

Preheat the grill to high. Grill the sausages, for 10–12 minutes, depending on their thickness, turning occasionally until cooked through. Thickly slice the sausages.

Meanwhile, heat half the olive oil in a wide, deep frying pan and fry the red pepper for 3 minutes until softened. Add the garlic and cook for a further minute. Add the tomatoes, thyme, paprika and butter beans and cook, for about 10 minutes, stirring regularly.

Add the spinach and a splash of water and cook until wilted, then stir in the mustard, lemon juice and sliced cooked sausages. Season with salt and pepper to taste and heat through.

Heat a large griddle pan. Brush the slices of bread with the remaining olive oil and griddle for 5 minutes, turning once, until slightly charred in places. (You may need to do this in two batches.) Serve the sausages and beans spooned on top of the griddled bread. Sprinkle the coriander leaves over before serving.

SAUSAGES WITH APPLE & ONION SEED CHUTNEY

Choose thick herby sausages with a high meat content for this comforting, one-pan dish. The sausages are immersed in a lightly spiced apple chutney so they take on its flavour. Great served with mash and green veg.

SERVES 4   PREPARATION TIME: 15 MINUTES   COOKING TIME: 35 MINUTES

8 fat herby sausages
2 tbsp olive oil
1 large onion, chopped
1 tsp onion seeds
3 apples, peeled, cored and diced
1 tbsp cider vinegar

1 tbsp thyme leaves, plus extra for
 sprinkling
1–2 tsp soft light brown sugar
1–2 tsp Dijon mustard
sea salt and freshly ground black pepper

Preheat the grill to medium-high. Grill the sausages for 15–18 minutes until browned all over.

Meanwhile, heat the olive oil in a wide, deep frying pan over a medium heat and cook the onion for 10 minutes until softened. Add the onion seeds and cook for 1 minute until they smell slightly toasted.

Add the apples, vinegar and 115ml/3¾fl oz/scant ½ cup water. Stir, cover and simmer for 15 minutes over a medium-low heat until the apples have softened.

Crush the apples with the back of a fork to break them down slightly and stir in the thyme, sugar and mustard, to taste. Season with salt and pepper.

Transfer the sausages to the pan and heat them in the chutney for 4–5 minutes, or until warmed through. Add a splash of water if the chutney looks too dry. Serve the sausages with the apple chutney, sprinkled with a few thyme leaves.

Choosing Sausages

Pork and apple are natural partners, with the sweet acidity of the fruit cutting through the rich fattiness of the sausages. Having said that, you can experiment with different types of sausages; try venison or lamb, or a vegetarian alternative. Or perhaps black pudding? Sausages with flavourings such as thyme, parsley, fennel seeds and garlic would also work well with the fruit chutney. Bear in mind that sausages do need a certain amount of fat, and breadcrumbs give them a lighter texture, so choose ones made with 80–90 per cent meat.

SLOW-COOKED MEXICAN PULLED PORK WITH PICKLED RED CABBAGE

This recipe needs a cut of pork such as a shoulder joint or leg. The pork is braised so slowly in a tangy, deeply intense barbecue sauce that it almost falls apart. Serve shredded with this red cabbage pickle, which, if made a few hours in advance, becomes vibrantly iridescent in colour.

**SERVES 4   PREPARATION TIME: 25 MINUTES, PLUS RESTING
COOKING TIME: 2 HOURS 20 MINUTES**

1.25kg/2lb 12oz pork shoulder, skin removed
1 tbsp sunflower oil
1 tsp smoked hot paprika
1 tsp English mustard powder
½ tsp ground ginger
4 tbsp tomato ketchup
2 tbsp cider vinegar
2 tsp Worcestershire sauce
½ tsp salt
2 tbsp dark muscovado sugar
1 large onion, cut into 8 wedges
juice of 1 large orange
1 handful of oregano sprigs

PICKLED RED CABBAGE:
100g/3½ oz red cabbage, shredded
1 large carrot, coarsely grated
2 tsp caster sugar
juice of 1 lime
2 tbsp cider vinegar
sea salt and freshly ground black pepper

TO SERVE:
8–12 tacos shells
shredded Little Gem lettuce
4 tbsp soured cream
1 small handful of coriander leaves

Preheat the oven to 150°C/300°F/Gas 2. Cut off as much fat as you can from the pork. Heat the oil in a large flameproof casserole and sear the pork over a medium heat until browned all over. Transfer the pork to a plate.

Mix together the smoked hot paprika, mustard powder, ginger, ketchup, vinegar, Worcestershire sauce, salt and sugar. Spread two-thirds of the mixture all over the pork. Put the onion in an even layer in the casserole and top it with the pork. Pour in the orange juice with 2 tablespoons water. Scatter the oregano over the top. Cover with a lid and roast for 2 hours, occasionally spooning the juices over the pork.

To make the pickle, put the cabbage and carrot in a serving bowl. Mix together the sugar, lime juice and vinegar until the sugar dissolves. Season and pour over the vegetables. Stir, then leave to one side.

After the pork has cooked for 2 hours, remove and discard the onions, then transfer the pork to a plate, cover with foil and leave to rest for 15 minutes. Increase the oven temperature to 180°C/350°F/Gas 4.

Put the casserole with the reserved sauce on the hob and pour in any juices from the resting joint. Bring to the boil, then reduce the heat and simmer until reduced by half and thickened. At the same time warm the taco shells for a few minutes in the oven. Using two forks, shred the pork into strips and discard any fat. Put the pork on a large serving plate, pour the sauce over and turn the meat until coated. Fill each taco with a little lettuce and top with the pork, a spoonful of soured cream, pickled cabbage and coriander leaves.

BAKED REDCURRANT & CLOVE GLAZED HAM

There is something magnificent about a baked ham with its glazed golden crust and succulent meat. Ham or the uncooked version, gammon, comes from the hind leg of the pig and is cured in much the same way as bacon. This recipe starts with cooking a gammon, but you can instead buy a ready-cooked joint, which may be sold as gammon ham. The ham is equally good served cold and thinly sliced as it is or served warm with roast potatoes.

**SERVES 4–6   PREPARATION TIME: 20 MINUTES, PLUS RESTING
COOKING TIME: 2 HOURS**

1.5kg/3lb 5oz smoked or unsmoked
  boneless gammon joint or ham joint
15 juniper berries, lightly crushed with
  the blade of a knife
2 bay leaves

3 tbsp redcurrant jelly
1 heaped tsp Dijon mustard
finely grated zest of 1 orange and juice
  of ½ orange
10–20 cloves, to taste

Put the gammon in a large lidded pan, cover with cold water and bring it slowly to the boil, then drain and discard the water.

Return the gammon to the pan, cover with fresh cold water and add the juniper berries and bay leaves. Bring to the boil again, then turn the heat down and simmer, part-covered, for 1 hour or until cooked. (Allow 20 minutes per 500g/1lb 2oz.) Drain the ham, discarding the juniper berries and bay leaves.

Twenty minutes before the gammon is cooked, preheat the oven to 200°C/400°F/Gas 6. Put the redcurrant jelly in a small pan with the mustard, orange zest and juice, stir, then simmer over a medium heat for about 10–15 minutes until reduced and thickened to a syrupy consistency.

Leave the ham to cool slightly, then remove and discard the skin, leaving an outer layer of fat. Pat the fat dry with kitchen paper, then use a sharp knife to score the meat diagonally. Change direction and score the fat in the opposite direction to form a diamond pattern. Press the cloves into the fat, making sure they are fairly evenly spaced, and spoon the redcurrant glaze over the top.

Put the ham into a roasting tin and bake for 25–30 minutes, basting the joint occasionally until the top is golden and caramelized. Remove from the oven, cover loosely with foil and leave to rest for 15 minutes before serving.

STEAK & ALE PIES

These individual beef and vegetable pot pies are topped with a type of hot-water crust pastry, which has a rich, golden exterior and crisp texture. This pastry crust differs from other versions of hot-water pastry in that it contains egg and butter instead of the usual lard so it has a softer texture, but more interestingly you leave it to cool before rolling out. The trick is to roll the pastry out between two sheets of cling film as this helps it to hold together and makes it more manageable. If time is against you, use ready-made puff pastry. Serve with mash — potato, celeriac, swede, squash or a combination of these — to soak up the delicious rich, boozy gravy.

MAKES 4   PREPARATION TIME: 30 MINUTES, PLUS CHILLING   COOKING TIME: 2¼ HOURS

PASTRY:
225g/8oz/heaped 1¾ cups plain flour
a pinch of salt
1 egg, plus 1 extra for glazing
75g/2½ oz butter

FILLING:
3–4 tbsp olive oil
850g/1lb 14oz braising steak, cut into
    bite-sized pieces, fat trimmed
2 tbsp plain flour

4 carrots, roughly chopped
300g/10½ oz baby button mushrooms
2 onions, sliced
3 garlic cloves, chopped
300ml/10½ fl oz/scant 1¼ cups ale
500ml/17fl oz/2 cups good-quality
    beef stock
2 tsp dried thyme
2 bay leaves
sea salt and freshly ground black pepper

To make the filling, heat 1 tablespoon of the olive oil in a flameproof casserole dish. Dust the beef in seasoned flour and sear in batches over a medium heat until browned all over. Add a little extra oil when necessary. Remove the beef using a slotted spoon and leave to one side.

Add another tablespoon of the oil to the casserole and fry the carrots and mushrooms for 5 minutes until softened and browned. Remove and leave to one side.

Add the remaining oil to the casserole, if needed, and fry the onions for 5 minutes, then add the garlic and cook for another minute until softened and golden.

Return the beef, carrots and mushrooms to the casserole and pour in the ale. Bring to the boil and cook until the ale has reduced by half. Add the stock, thyme and bay leaves and stir until combined. Return to the boil, then turn the heat down and simmer, covered, for 1 hour.

Remove the casserole lid, stir, and continue to simmer the stew for 30 minutes until the beef is tender and the gravy has reduced and thickened. Season to taste.

While the beef is cooking, make the pastry. Sift the flour and salt into a mixing bowl. Make a well in the centre and add the egg. Put the butter and 100ml/3½fl oz/generous ⅓ cup water in a pan and heat gently, stirring occasionally, until the butter has melted, then bring the mixture to the boil.

CONTINUED ON PAGE **42**

Pour the pastry mixture into the bowl containing the flour and mix with a wooden spoon to form a sticky dough. Tip the dough onto a large plate, spread out using the back of the wooden spoon and leave to cool for about 10 minutes.

Knead the dough into a ball (it's similar to a sticky paste and should hold together), then wrap in cling film. Chill for 30 minutes to firm up.

Preheat the oven to 220°C/425°F/Gas 7. Divide the beef filling into four 10cm/4in deep individual pie dishes and put on a large baking sheet.

Divide the pastry into 5 equal pieces. To make the pie tops, roll out 4 pieces between sheets of cling film into ovals, each about 1cm/½in larger than the top of the dish. Roll out the remaining piece of dough and cut it into 4 strips, each the width of a dish rim and long enough to fit around the top of a dish.

Lightly beat the remaining egg, then brush a little over the top of each dish. Lay a pastry strip around the edge of a dish and brush with more egg. Drape the pastry oval on top and press the edges together to seal. Trim off any excess pastry, then crimp the edges. Repeat to make 4 pies and brush the pastry with the remaining egg. Prick the tops a few times with a fork and decorate with any surplus pastry, if you like.

Bake for 10 minutes, then reduce the oven temperature to 200°C/400°F/Gas 6 and cook for another 20–25 minutes until the pastry is golden and cooked through.

Braising Steak

These pies require a cut of steak or beef that becomes succulent and tender when slow-cooked over a gentle heat. Perfect for this are the parts of the cow that do the most work, such as the legs, shoulder (chuck), shin or rump. Often labelled as stewing or braising steak, these cuts can be tough and need long, slow cooking to become tender, but they are usually the most flavourful. When buying braising steak, look for a good marbling of fat running through the meat; it will break down during cooking and add lots of flavour.

In contrast, cuts from parts of the cow that get little exercise, such as the fillet or sirloin, have the best texture and flavour when cooked briefly (pan-fried, grilled or roasted) using a high heat.

VENISON WELLINGTON

Perfect for a dinner party or special occasion, this venison fillet wrapped in puff pastry has layers of prosciutto, mushroom duxelles and chicken liver parfait – and it makes a spectacular centrepiece. If you can't find venison, and for a slightly more economic alternative, you can choose beef fillet instead. Mushroom duxelles is similar to a coarse pâté and can also be served as a starter on thin slices of toast.

**SERVES 6–8 PREPARATION TIME: 25 MINUTES, PLUS SOAKING, COOLING AND RESTING
COOKING TIME: 1 HOUR 5 MINUTES**

olive oil, for brushing
900g/2lb venison fillet, trimmed of fat
375g/13oz block puff pastry
flour, for dusting
1 small egg, beaten
100g/3½ oz prosciutto
175g/6oz chicken liver parfait
sea salt and freshly ground black pepper

MUSHROOM DUXELLES:
20g/¾oz dried porcini mushrooms
50g/1¾oz butter
400g/14oz field mushrooms, finely
  chopped
4 thyme sprigs, leaves removed
5 tbsp fresh white breadcrumbs

Cover the porcini mushrooms with just-boiled water and leave for 20 minutes to soften. Meanwhile, brush the olive oil all over the venison and season with salt and pepper. Heat a wide, deep frying pan over a high heat and sear the venison until browned all over. Put it on a rack over a plate and leave to cool.

To make the mushroom duxelles, drain the porcini (reserving the soaking liquor), squeeze out any excess water and finely chop. Melt the butter in the same pan used for the venison. Add the porcini and field mushrooms and cook over a medium heat for 20 minutes, stirring until softened and there is no trace of liquid. Season and stir in the thyme and breadcrumbs. Transfer to a large shallow bowl and leave to cool.

Preheat the oven to 200°C/400°F/Gas 6. Line a baking sheet with baking paper. Cut a third off the block of pastry and roll it out on a lightly floured work surface until about 5cm/2in wider and longer than the venison. Put the pastry on the lined baking sheet and brush it with beaten egg.

Put a layer of the prosciutto about the same size as the venison on top of the pastry. Top with the venison and spread the chicken liver parfait over the meat in an even layer. Spoon the mushroom duxelles over the top, pressing it so that it sticks to the parfait.

Roll out the remaining pastry on a lightly floured work surface until large enough to cover the mushroom-coated venison. Brush the pastry surrounding the filling with more of the beaten egg and drape the pastry over the top. Press the edges of the pastry together around the filling to seal it, then trim any excess. Crimp the edges with a fork and prick the top of the Wellington in several places. Decorate with any spare pastry.

Brush the Wellington with the remaining beaten egg. Bake for 20 minutes, then reduce the oven temperature to 180°C/350°F/Gas 4 and bake for another 10 minutes until the pastry is golden and cooked through. Remove from the oven and leave to stand for 10 minutes before slicing.

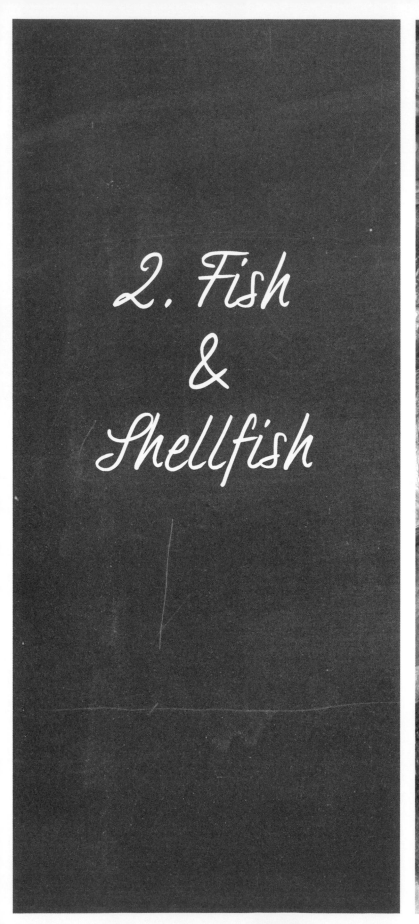

2. Fish & Shellfish

Fresh Marinated Anchovies

Marinated pickled anchovies are a familiar sight in deli chiller cabinets. Here, the small, slender fish are preserved in vinegar and flavoured with garlic, red onion and parsley until lightly cured.

SERVES 4–6   PREPARATION TIME: 1 HOUR, PLUS 2 DAYS MARINATING

300g/10½ oz fresh anchovies, sprats or small sardines, rinsed and patted dry
1 tbsp sea salt
6 tbsp white wine vinegar
2 garlic cloves, cut into thin slivers
2 tbsp lemon juice
2 tbsp extra virgin olive oil
½ small red onion, diced
2 tbsp chopped flat-leaf parsley leaves

Cut the anchovies down the belly and open up each fish. To remove the backbone, run your finger down it, separating the flesh from the bone and gently prising it out. Remove the head and tail and lift out the backbone. Continue until all the fish are filleted; you should have whole, butterflied fillets.

Put the anchovies, flesh upwards, in a single layer in a non-metallic dish and sprinkle lightly with the salt. Mix the vinegar with 1 tablespoon water and spoon the mixture over the anchovies. Scatter the garlic over, cover the dish with cling film and refrigerate for 48 hours. The fish will marinate and turn white.

Drain the anchovies and discard the liquid. Rinse them briefly under cold running water, pat dry and put them in a clean dish. Spoon the lemon juice and olive oil over them and sprinkle with the red onion and parsley. The fish are ready to eat straight away but will keep for 1 week in the fridge in an airtight container.

PISSALADIÈRE WITH **MARINATED ANCHOVIES**

This Provençal variation of the classic Italian pizza is topped with a generous amount of slowly cooked onions as well as anchovies, olives and thyme. The marinated fresh anchovies are a twist on the traditional thin, brown, salted ones.

SERVES 6   PREPARATION TIME: 20 MINUTES, PLUS RISING   COOKING TIME: 1¼ HOURS

250g/9oz/2 cups plain flour, plus extra
   for dusting
1 tsp salt
1½ tsp easy-blend dried yeast
½ tsp sugar
1 egg, lightly beaten
3 tbsp olive oil, plus extra for greasing

1kg/2lb 4oz Spanish onions, thinly sliced
2 large garlic cloves, crushed
1 tbsp thyme leaves
6 Fresh Marinated Anchovies (see page 46),
   halved lengthways into thin strips
1 handful of black olives
freshly ground black pepper

To make the dough, mix together the flour, salt, yeast and sugar in a large mixing bowl. Add the egg, 1 tablespoon of the olive oil and 5 tablespoons tepid water. Mix until the dough comes together, adding a little more water if the dough is too dry. Turn out the dough on a lightly floured work surface and knead for 5 minutes until it comes together into a smooth ball. Put the dough in a lightly oiled bowl, cover with cling film and leave to rise while you cook the onions.

Heat the remaining olive oil in a large, non-stick frying pan over a medium heat. Add the onions, turn the heat down to low, and cook, covered with a lid for 30 minutes, stirring occasionally until the onions are meltingly soft but not coloured. Remove the lid 10 minutes before the end of the cooking time to reduce any liquid in the pan. Add the garlic and fry for another minute. Remove from the heat and leave to cool slightly.

Preheat the oven to 220°C/425°F/Gas 7. Lightly oil a large, shallow, non-stick baking tray, about 26 x 40cm/ 10½ x 16in. Roll out the dough and use to line the baking tray, pressing the dough up the sides.

Spoon the onion mixture on top of the dough, sprinkle with the thyme, then arrange the anchovies on top in a criss-cross pattern. Season with pepper and top with the olives. Bake for 25–30 minutes until the base is cooked and golden. Serve warm, cut into wedges.

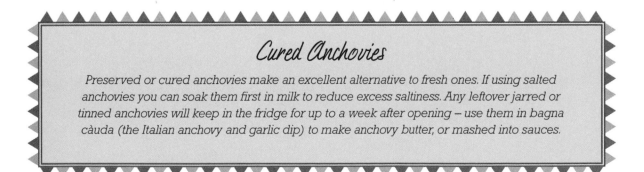

Cured Anchovies

Preserved or cured anchovies make an excellent alternative to fresh ones. If using salted anchovies you can soak them first in milk to reduce excess saltiness. Any leftover jarred or tinned anchovies will keep in the fridge for up to a week after opening – use them in bagna càuda (the Italian anchovy and garlic dip) to make anchovy butter, or mashed into sauces.

Crab Terrine

The combination of white and brown crabmeat gives this simple terrine a delicious flavour and texture. Light as a feather, the creamy terrine makes the perfect topping for thin and crisp slices of Melba toast, crostini or crackers. Alternatively, serve with a crisp green salad and crusty bread for a more substantial lunch.

**SERVES 8–10   PREPARATION TIME: 25 MINUTES, PLUS CHILLING
COOKING TIME: 5 MINUTES**

250ml/9fl oz/1 cup good-quality fish stock
1½ sachets of gelatine granules, about 15g/½ oz total weight
450g/1lb crabmeat, half white and half brown meat
2 tbsp lemon juice
a good dash of Tabasco sauce
½ tsp sea salt
250ml/9fl oz/1 cup crème fraîche
1 large egg white
freshly ground white pepper
paprika, for dusting

MELBA TOAST:
slices of day-old wholemeal or white bread

Heat the stock in a small saucepan and stir in the gelatine until the granules dissolve.
Leave to cool slightly until the gelatine just begins to set.

Mix the white and brown crabmeat together in a large mixing bowl. Fold in the gelatine mixture, lemon juice, Tabasco, salt and crème fraîche until combined, taking care not to break up the crabmeat too much.

Whisk the egg white in a clean, grease-free bowl until it forms stiff peaks, then using a metal spoon fold it into the crabmeat mixture. Season with white pepper. Pour the mixture into a 900g/2lb terrine or dish, cover with cling film and put in the fridge to set. It will take a few hours to firm up and set to a light, mousse-like texture. Before serving, turn the terrine out onto a serving plate and dust the top with paprika. The terrine will keep for up to 3 days in the fridge.

To make the Melba toast, preheat the grill to high. Toast the bread until golden on both sides and then cut off the crusts. Carefully cut each slice of toast horizontally into 2 thin pieces, then cut each piece diagonally into two triangles. Reduce the grill to medium and grill the untoasted side of each triangular piece of bread until golden and crisp. Leave to cool before serving with the terrine.

CREAMY **CRAB TERRINE** & SPRING ONION TART

If you have any leftover Crab Terrine, why not use it as the base of a seafood tart, flavoured with thin slices of spring onion and flecks of red chilli? You don't want the chillies to be too hot, but just hot enough to cut through the richness of the crab and add a slight kick.

SERVES 6   PREPARATION TIME: 30 MINUTES, PLUS CHILLING   COOKING TIME: 55 MINUTES

PASTRY:
200g/7oz/scant 1⅔ cups plain flour, plus
    extra for dusting
a large pinch of salt
90g/3¼ oz cold butter, cubed, plus extra
    for greasing
1 egg yolk, beaten

FILLING:
1 tbsp olive oil
3 spring onions, finely chopped
2 red chillies, deseeded and finely
    chopped
200g/7oz Crab Terrine (see page 48)
4 large eggs, lightly beaten
200ml/7fl oz/scant 1 cup whole milk
150g/5½ oz white crabmeat
sea salt and freshly ground black pepper

First make the pastry. Sift the flour and salt into a mixing bowl and rub in the butter with your fingertips until you have a mixture that resembles coarse breadcrumbs. Using a table knife, stir in the egg yolk and enough water, about 2 tablespoons, to bring the mixture together. Alternatively, you can use a food processor to make the pastry.

Tip the dough onto a lightly floured work surface and form into a smooth ball. Wrap in cling film, flatten slightly into a disc and chill for 30 minutes.

Preheat the oven to 190°C/375°F/Gas 5 and lightly grease a 25cm/10in flan tin with butter. Roll out the pastry on a lightly floured surface and use to line the prepared flan tin. Leave the excess to hang over the edge of the tin. Prick the base with a fork and line the pastry with baking paper and baking beans and bake blind for 15 minutes. Remove the baking beans and paper and bake for a further 10 minutes until the pastry is cooked and light golden. Reduce the oven temperature to 170°C/325°F/Gas 3.

Remove the pastry case from the oven and trim the edges. Meanwhile, make the filling. Heat the olive oil and fry the spring onions and chillies over a medium heat for 2–3 minutes until softened. Leave to cool.

In a large bowl, mix the crab terrine into the beaten eggs and milk until combined. Stir in the white crabmeat, spring onions and chilli. Season with salt and pepper and pour the mixture into the pastry-lined dish. Bake for 30 minutes until just firm. Leave to cool slightly before serving.

WARM SQUID & CHORIZO SALAD

To prepare a succulent squid you need either to cook it over a low heat for a generous period of time or quickly over a fairly high heat. In this recipe, the squid needs to be cooked very briefly – just a minute or so in a hot griddle pan will ensure it is beautifully tender. Any leftover garlic and herb oil will keep in the fridge for up to 1 week.

SERVES 4   PREPARATION TIME: 25 MINUTES   COOKING TIME: 20 MINUTES

650g/1lb 7oz squid
extra virgin olive oil, for frying
125g/4½ oz chorizo, thickly sliced
100g/3½ oz wild rocket leaves
crusty bread, to serve

GARLIC AND HERB OIL:
125ml/4fl oz/½ cup extra virgin olive oil
juice of ½ lemon

2 garlic cloves, preferably new season, crushed
1 red chilli, deseeded and finely chopped
1 handful of flat-leaf parsley, finely chopped
3 basil sprigs, leaves torn into small pieces
sea salt and freshly ground black pepper

To make the garlic and herb oil, pour the olive oil into a jug and whisk in the lemon juice. Next, stir in the garlic, chilli, parsley and basil, then season with salt and pepper. Leave to one side until ready to serve.

To prepare the squid, remove the intestines by pulling the tentacles and insides away from the body. Cut the tentacles just below the eyes and leave to one side. Discard the eyes and intestines. Pull out the plastic-like quill from the body cavity and discard. Wash out the body to remove any remaining entrails. Peel off any exterior browny-pink skin, then rinse the squid again.

Cut the squid into 5cm/2in pieces and lightly score the inside of each piece with the tip of a small, sharp knife. Cover and refrigerate the squid and tentacles until needed.

Heat a splash of olive oil in a frying pan over a medium heat and cook the chorizo for about 3 minutes, turning once, until almost crisp. Remove from the pan and drain on kitchen paper. Cut into small bite-sized pieces and leave to one side.

Heat a large griddle pan until very hot over a high heat. Brush the pieces of squid with a little oil and griddle them for about 30 seconds on each side, pressing the squid onto the hot ridges of the pan, until opaque and marked by the grill. You will need to do this in batches.

Lay the squid on a bed of rocket with the chorizo on a serving plate, spoon the garlic and herb oil over the top and serve immediately with crusty bread.

HOT MACKEREL NIÇOISE

This is a twist on the classic Provençal salad, using flakes of hot smoked mackerel instead of the usual tinned tuna.

SERVES 4   PREPARATION TIME: 30 MINUTES   COOKING TIME: 20 MINUTES

500g/1lb 2oz new potatoes, scrubbed and halved if large
2 large eggs
5 large vine-ripened tomatoes
125g/4½ oz French beans, trimmed
100g/3½ oz watercress
1 Sweet Gem lettuce, leaves separated and large leaves sliced
½ cucumber, quartered lengthways, deseeded and cut into chunks
1 small red onion, cut into thin rings
55g/2oz black olives, such as Kalamata olives
1 small handful of flat-leaf parsley, leaves roughly chopped
350g/12oz smoked mackerel fillets

DRESSING:
½ tsp sea salt flakes
1 garlic clove
1 tsp English mustard powder
1 tbsp white wine vinegar
100ml/3½ fl oz/generous ⅓ cup extra virgin olive oil
2 tbsp snipped chives
freshly ground black pepper

Cook the potatoes in a pan of boiling salted water for 15 minutes until tender. Drain and leave to one side.

Meanwhile, boil the eggs for 8 minutes until the white is set and the yolk is still slightly runny. Drain and cool slightly under cold running water, then peel and slice into quarters.

Using a small, sharp knife, cut a shallow cross in the bottom of each tomato, then put them in a heatproof bowl and cover with just-boiled water. Leave to stand for 2 minutes, then drain. Peel off and discard the tomato skins, then deseed and cut the flesh into large chunks. Leave to one side.

Steam the French beans for 5 minutes until just tender, then refresh briefly under cold running water; you still want them to be slightly warm and crisp.

To make the dressing, pound the salt flakes and garlic to a paste using a pestle and mortar. Stir in the mustard powder, then add the vinegar and stir until the salt dissolves. Pour in the olive oil and whisk with a fork until combined. Stir in the chives, season with pepper and leave to one side.

Put the watercress and lettuce in a large serving bowl and scatter the tomatoes, cucumber, red onion, olives and parsley over. Top with the green beans. Pour half of the dressing over and toss the salad until combined.

Heat a large frying pan over a medium heat and warm through the mackerel for 3 minutes, turning once, until slightly crisp on the surface. Remove the mackerel from the heat and peel away the skin. Cut the mackerel fillets into large flakes and put on top of the salad with the eggs, then drizzle more of the dressing over to taste and serve while still warm.

SMOKED FISH & COCKLE CHOWDER

Evaporated milk is the surprise ingredient in this chowder, adding a rich creaminess to the sauce. You could serve the chowder, as is the custom in San Francisco, in large hollowed-out sourdough rolls. If you can't find cockles, use clams from a jar.

SERVES 4   PREPARATION TIME: 15 MINUTES   COOKING TIME: 25 MINUTES

600g/1lb 5oz undyed smoked haddock
   fillets
400ml/14fl oz/generous 1½ cups milk
1 tbsp sunflower oil
2 smoked streaky bacon rashers,
   cut into small pieces
2 onions, finely chopped
1 bay leaf
2 carrots, diced

300g/10½ oz potatoes, peeled and diced
800ml/28fl oz/scant 3½ cups good-quality
   fish or vegetable stock
4 tbsp evaporated milk
280g/10oz bottled cockles, drained and
   rinsed well, especially if they are in
   vinegar
freshly ground black pepper
chopped chives, for sprinkling

Put the haddock flesh-side down in a large, deep frying pan and pour the milk over the top. Bring to the boil, turn the heat down to low and simmer for 8 minutes until the fish is just cooked. Remove the haddock with a spatula, transfer to a plate and leave to one side. Strain the milk in the pan into a jug, discarding any solids, and leave to one side.

Meanwhile, heat the sunflower oil in a large saucepan and fry the bacon for 2 minutes until beginning to brown, then add the onions and cook for another 5 minutes until the onion has softened. Stir in the bay leaf, carrots and potatoes and cook for a further 5 minutes.

Pour the stock into the pan and bring to the boil, then turn the heat down to low and simmer, part-covered, for 10 minutes until the carrots and potatoes are tender.

While the vegetables are cooking, remove and discard the skin and bones from the haddock fillets, then flake the flesh into large chunks. Add the reserved milk, evaporated milk, cooked haddock and cockles to the saucepan. Season with pepper (you are unlikely to need salt as the fish is quite salty) and heat for a few minutes. Serve sprinkled with chives.

Smoked Fish

Commercial smokeries tend to use a "smoke" dye rather than actually smoking the fish; the vivid yellow or orange colour of the so-called smoked fish is a telltale sign. Preferably, look for undyed fish, which is, not surprisingly, paler in colour.

Salmon Gravadlax with Lemon & Ginger

Make sure you use the freshest salmon when making gravadlax, and ideally you should aim for a mid-cut fillet, not as thin as the tail end and not too thick to take on the flavours of the marinade. Finely grated lemon zest and fresh root ginger make a flavourful alternative to this recipe's more standard use of dill.

SERVES 4 AS A LIGHT MEAL OR 6 AS A STARTER
PREPARATION TIME: 15 MINUTES, PLUS 2 DAYS MARINATING

500g/1lb 2oz salmon fillet
85g/3oz/heaped ⅓ cup rock salt
85g/3oz/heaped ⅓ cup granulated sugar
finely grated zest of 2 lemons
2.5cm/1in piece of fresh root ginger, peeled and grated
1 tbsp lemon juice
freshly ground black pepper (optional)

Using a pair of tweezers, remove any bones from the salmon. Lay the salmon, flesh-side down, in a non-metallic dish. Mix the salt and sugar together and sprinkle half the mixture over the skin in an even layer, then turn the salmon over and sprinkle with the remaining salt and sugar mixture, making sure the fish is completely covered. Cover the dish with cling film. Put a plate on top of the salmon and weight it down to encourage the curing process. Leave in the fridge for 24 hours, turning after 12 hours.

Remove the salmon from the fridge and wipe away all the salt and sugar. Gently rinse under lightly running cold water, then pat dry and return the salmon to the dry, clean dish.

Mix the lemon zest and ginger together and scatter them over the salmon until covered, pressing the flavourings into the flesh, then sprinkle sparingly with the lemon juice. Season with pepper, if using. Cover the dish with cling film and refrigerate for 24 hours.

When ready to serve, remove the salmon from the fridge and cut into thin slices on the diagonal. The gravadlax will keep for up to 4 days stored in the fridge.

SALMON GRAVADLAX SUSHI

This sushi recipe doesn't require any complex or fiddly rolling techniques and is surprisingly simple to make. The cured salmon flavoured with lemon and ginger makes a refreshing change to the usual raw salmon, but that's not to say it doesn't taste authentic thanks to the seasoned sushi rice, potent wasabi paste and toasted nori sheets.

**MAKES 20 SQUARES   PREPARATION TIME: 20 MINUTES, PLUS STANDING,
COOLING AND CHILLING   COOKING TIME: 10 MINUTES**

270g/9½ oz/generous 1¼ cups sushi rice
2½ tbsp rice wine vinegar
1 tsp sea salt
2½ tsp caster sugar
225g/8oz Salmon Gravadlax with Lemon
   & Ginger (see page 56), or smoked
   salmon, cut into thin slices

2 tsp wasabi paste
1¼ sheets of toasted nori
Japanese soy sauce and pickled ginger,
   to serve

Cover the rice with water in a bowl and leave to stand for 20 minutes, then drain and rinse well. Transfer the rice to a pan and cover with 400ml/14fl oz/generous 1½ cups water. Bring to the boil, then turn the heat down to very low, cover and simmer for about 10 minutes, or until the water has been absorbed. Remove from the heat and leave to stand, covered, for 10 minutes.

Mix together the rice wine vinegar, salt and sugar in a small bowl. Transfer the cooked rice to a large, shallow tray and spread it out. Spoon the vinegar mixture over the rice and mix gently until the rice is coated. Leave the rice to cool.

Line a 23cm/9in tin with cling film, leaving sufficient excess to fold over the top. Arrange the salmon slices, overlapping each other slightly, to cover the base of the lined tin. Put dots of the wasabi over the fish, then, using a wet knife, spread the rice in an even layer over the top. Press the rice down to make a firm layer.

Finish with a single layer of nori (you may need to cut them with scissors to fit) then fold the surplus cling film over the top to cover. Put a piece of cardboard on top and weight it down. Chill for 1 hour, then remove the weight and cardboard, and using a wet-bladed knife cut into 20 squares. Serve with soy sauce and pickled ginger.

SHELLFISH LINGUINE WITH CRISPY CAPERS

A real treat of a dish made with a mixture of fresh seafood, including clams, mussels and cockles. Choose the small capers in brine that you find in jars and drain and rinse them well before use.

SERVES 4   PREPARATION TIME: 30 MINUTES   COOKING TIME: 15 MINUTES

1.3kg/3lb mixed shellfish, including clams, cockles and mussels in the shell

2½ tbsp olive oil

2 tbsp small capers, drained, rinsed and patted dry

350g/12oz dried linguine

5 garlic cloves, finely chopped

5 large vine-ripened tomatoes, quartered, deseeded and chopped

1 red chilli, deseeded and finely chopped

4 tbsp chopped parsley leaves

350ml/12fl oz/scant 1½ cups dry white wine

freshly ground black pepper

Discard any shellfish with broken shells or those that remain open when tapped. Scrub and clean the shellfish, pulling out the beard from the mussels. Rinse well in plenty of cold running water.

Heat ½ tablespoon of the olive oil in a frying pan and fry the capers for 2–3 minutes or until crisp. Drain on kitchen paper and leave to one side. Bring a large saucepan of salted water to the boil and cook the linguine following the instructions on the packet until al dente. Drain the pasta and keep warm.

Meanwhile, heat the remaining olive oil in a large saucepan over a medium heat. Cook the garlic, tomatoes, chilli and half of the parsley for 2 minutes, then pour in the wine. Bring to the boil and boil for 2 minutes or until there is no aroma of alcohol. Add the shellfish to the pan, cover and cook for 4–5 minutes, shaking the pan occasionally until the shells open. Discard any that remain closed.

Remove half of the shellfish from their shells. Toss the pasta and the shelled shellfish into the pan and season with black pepper; you are unlikely to need salt. Add the shellfish in their shells to the pan and serve immediately sprinkled with the crisp capers and remaining parsley.

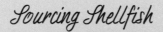

Sourcing Shellfish

The term "shellfish" covers a wealth of seafood from molluscs, including mussels, scallops, razor clams, oysters, clams and cockles, to crustaceans such as crabs, lobsters and prawns. When making this pasta dish, look for super-fresh live shellfish, with smooth, shiny shells that are tight shut or shut immediately after tapping them. Discard any that remain closed after cooking.

Potted Shrimps

For convenience this recipe uses peeled brown shrimps – these tiny shrimps are tiresomely fiddly to peel, and if you are starting from scratch you'll need about 600g/1lb 5oz unpeeled shrimps. But it's worth it – in spite of their diminutive size, brown shrimps are packed with flavour.

SERVES 4   PREPARATION TIME: 15 MINUTES, PLUS CHILLING

115g/4oz butter
200g/7oz cooked peeled brown shrimps
2 tsp lemon juice
¼ tsp ground mace
¼ tsp cayenne pepper
sea salt and freshly ground black pepper
thin slices of toast, to serve

Melt the butter in a small pan over a medium-low heat. When it has melted, add the shrimps and stir them in the butter for 30 seconds, then remove the pan from the heat.

Stir in the lemon juice, mace and cayenne and season with salt. Add more seasoning to taste, if required. Using a slotted spoon, divide the shrimps into four ramekins, then pour the butter over to just cover. Press the shrimps down into the melted butter slightly, then leave to cool.

Transfer the potted shrimps to the fridge to firm up and cover with cling film until ready to serve. They will keep for up to 3 days. Remove from the fridge 30 minutes before serving to allow the butter to soften slightly. Serve with thin slices of toast.

SEA BREAM WITH **POTTED SHRIMPS** IN BUTTER SAUCE

Sea bream is an excellent fish in this recipe because its light, delicate flesh works well with the buttery, lemony sauce and the intense flavour of the brown shrimps.

SERVES 4   **PREPARATION TIME: 10 MINUTES**   **COOKING TIME: 5 MINUTES**

4 sea bream fillets
flour, for dusting
70g/2½ oz butter
½ recipe quantity Potted Shrimps,
  about 250g/9oz (see page 60)

juice of 1 large lemon
sea salt and freshly ground black pepper
lemon wedges, boiled new potatoes and
  steamed spinach, to serve

Lightly dust the fillets of bream in seasoned flour. Melt the butter in a large frying pan over a medium-high heat. When hot and sizzling, add the bream, flesh-side down, and cook for 3 minutes, turning once, until slightly golden and almost cooked.

Add the potted shrimps and cook for another minute, spooning the buttery sauce over the fish.

Squeeze in the lemon juice and heat through briefly, continuing to spoon the sauce over the bream. Season and serve the fish with the potted shrimp sauce spooned over the top, and with lemon wedges, new potatoes and spinach.

SPANISH STUFFED SQUID

Calasparra paella rice is a favourite here as its short grains readily take on the flavours of the vegetables, wine, stock and squid without losing their shape. It's important to cook the squid low and slow until so tender you can almost cut them with a fork.

SERVES 4   PREPARATION TIME: 30 MINUTES   COOKING TIME: 1½ HOURS

12 medium squid
a large pinch of saffron threads
4 large vine-ripened tomatoes
2 tbsp olive oil
1 large onion, chopped
1 romano red pepper, deseeded and chopped
3 large garlic cloves, finely chopped

350g/12oz/scant 1⅔ cups Calasparra paella rice
270ml/9½ fl oz/generous 1 cup dry white wine
650ml/22½ fl oz/generous 2½ cups good-quality hot chicken stock
1 tsp mild smoked paprika
sea salt and freshly ground black pepper
chopped parsley leaves, for sprinkling

To prepare the squid, remove the intestines by pulling the tentacles and insides away from the body. Cut the tentacles just below the eyes and leave to one side for use in another dish. Discard the eyes and intestines. Pull out the plastic-like quill from the body cavity and discard. Wash out the body to remove any remaining entrails. Peel off any exterior browny-pink skin, then rinse the squid again and leave to one side.

Soak the saffron threads in a little just-boiled water and leave to one side until ready to use.

Using a small, sharp knife, cut a shallow cross in the bottom of each tomato, then put them in a heatproof bowl and cover with just-boiled water. Leave to stand for 2 minutes, then drain. Peel off and discard the tomato skins, then deseed and cut the flesh into large chunks. Strain the seeds and juices into a bowl.

Heat half of the olive oil in a large, heavy-based frying pan over a medium heat. Cook the onion for 5 minutes until softened. Add the romano pepper and garlic and cook for another 3 minutes until tender. Add the rice and stir until the rice is glossy. Pour in 170ml/5½fl oz/⅔ cup of the wine, stir and cook until it is absorbed. Add half of the tomatoes, the saffron water, the stock and smoked paprika and stir until combined, then turn the heat down to low and simmer for 20 minutes, stirring occasionally, until the rice is just tender. Season well with salt and pepper.

Preheat the oven to 180°C/350°F/Gas 4. Using a teaspoon, stuff the paella into the squid, pressing it down to the pointed tip (you want the squid to be as full as possible), then secure with a wooden cocktail stick. Repeat until all the squid are stuffed.

Put the squid in a large ovenproof dish, then mix together the tomato juices, the remaining diced tomato, olive oil, wine and 6 tablespoons water. Spoon the mixture over the squid, season with salt and pepper, cover the dish with foil and bake for 50–55 minutes until the squid is very tender. Serve the squid with the tomatoey juices spooned over the top, a twist of black pepper and a sprinkling of parsley.

VODKA-CURED SALMON

The salmon is cured briefly, just enough to give it a firm texture and good flavour, so this is a perfect recipe for a quick supper. Try to use thick salmon fillets as they work best.

SERVES 4   PREPARATION TIME: 30 MINUTES, PLUS CHILLING   COOKING TIME: 5 MINUTES

40g/1½ oz/scant ¼ cup sea salt flakes
55g/2oz/¼ cup caster sugar
4 thick salmon fillets, skin removed, about
   175g/6oz each
100ml/3½ fl oz/generous ⅓ cup vodka
25g/1oz butter
2 tsp olive oil

125ml/4fl oz/½ cup crème fraîche
juice of ½ lemon
freshly ground black pepper
Sweet Cucumber Relish (see page 21)
   or cucumber pickle, to serve
samphire or green beans and crusty
   bread, to serve

To prepare the salmon, mix together the salt and sugar in a bowl. Lay the salmon in a shallow dish and pour the vodka over. Spoon any vodka in the bottom of the dish over the fillets and repeat this a few times. Sprinkle the salt and sugar over the top of the salmon and rub it in until the salmon is evenly covered. Cover the dish with cling film and chill for 2 hours.

Scrape the salt and sugar off the salmon and rinse it briefly under cold running water. Pat dry thoroughly.

Heat the butter and olive oil in a large, non-stick frying pan over a medium heat. Season the salmon with pepper and cook for about 2 minutes on each side.

Meanwhile, mix together the crème fraîche and lemon juice and season with pepper. Serve the salmon with the lemony crème fraîche spooned over the top with Sweet Cucumber Relish, samphire and crusty bread.

Curing Fish

Before the days of refrigeration, curing became an essential method of preservation to extend the natural shelf life of fish as well as a way of storing a glut of seafood. There are various methods of curing fish – salting, drying, smoking and pickling, or a combination of these techniques. For instance, salmon is usually cured first before being hot or cold smoked. Curing also influences the flavour and texture of seafood. When curing, use only the freshest fish or seafood you can buy – ideally those that smell pleasantly of the sea.

BLACKENED FISH WITH COUSCOUS & FRESH COCONUT RELISH

The coconut relish is full of fresh, zingy flavours and vibrant colour and is the perfect match for the crisp, spice-crusted fish. The relative blandness of the couscous is just the right foil for this flavour-packed dish. Use a wholemeal couscous if you can.

SERVES 4   PREPARATION TIME: 30 MINUTES   COOKING TIME: 10 MINUTES

175g/6oz/scant 1 cup wholemeal
   couscous
1 tsp vegetable bouillon powder
40g/1½ oz butter
2 tsp ground coriander
1 tsp ground cumin
1 tsp sumac
1 tsp dried thyme
4 thick white fish fillets, about
   175g/6oz each
1 tbsp olive oil
sea salt and freshly ground black pepper

COCONUT RELISH:
55g/2oz unsweetened desiccated coconut
juice of 1 large lime
1 large handful of mint leaves, roughly
   chopped
1 large handful of coriander leaves,
   roughly chopped
1 tsp caster sugar
1 green chilli, deseeded and finely
   chopped

To make the coconut relish, mix together all the ingredients in a non-metallic bowl. Season with salt and leave to one side to allow the flavours to merge together.

Put the couscous in a bowl and pour over just-boiled water to cover by 1cm/½in. Stir in the vegetable bouillon, cover and leave for 5 minutes, or until the stock is absorbed. Using a fork, stir in 25g/1oz of the butter, fluffing up the grains.

Meanwhile, mix together the ground coriander, cumin, sumac and thyme. Season with salt and pepper and sprinkle the mixture over the top of each fish fillet. Press the spices into the fish until evenly coated.

Heat the remaining butter and olive oil in a large, non-stick frying pan over a medium heat. When the butter has melted, add the fish, spice-side down first, and cook for about 2½ minutes on each side. Serve the fish with the couscous, topped with a spoonful of the coconut relish.

Home-Smoked Trout

Home-smoking is immensely satisfying and surprisingly simple, especially since you don't need any special kitchen equipment. A lidded wok is used here, but you could try a heavy roasting tin or charcoal barbecue. The smoking mixture lends a subtle smokiness to the fish, which works particularly well with the delicate flavour of the trout.

SERVES 4   PREPARATION TIME: 15 MINUTES   COOKING TIME: 18 MINUTES

4 large trout fillets
vegetable oil, for greasing
salt and freshly ground black pepper

SMOKING MIXTURE:
3 large handfuls of white rice
1 large handful of Earl Grey tea leaves
2 tbsp soft light brown sugar

Rinse and pat dry the trout fillets, then season with salt and pepper.

To prepare the smoker, line the base and lid of a wok with foil. Put the work on a wok stand, if you have one, to keep it stable. Mix together the rice, tea leaves and sugar in the base of the wok. Lightly grease a wire rack and put it over the top of the smoking mixture, making sure it does not touch.

Put the trout, skin side-down, on the rack and cover with the foil-lined lid. Heat the wok over a medium heat until you start to see little wisps of smoke escaping around the lid. Carefully patch up any leaks with foil, turn the heat down to medium-low and make sure the kitchen is well ventilated.

Smoke the trout for 18 minutes or until the fish is opaque. Make sure the mixture in the wok continues to smoke during this time. Turn off the heat and when the smoke has subsided, remove the lid. Using a fish slice, transfer the trout to serving plates.

SMOKED TROUT WITH POTATO LATKES & BEETROOT RELISH

Inspired by Jewish cuisine, the lightly smoked, delicate fillets of trout are perfect with the crisp, golden potato latkes and slightly sweet roasted beetroot coated in a horseradish cream sauce.

SERVES 4   PREPARATION TIME: 20 MINUTES   COOKING TIME: 55 MINUTES

1 recipe quantity Home-Smoked Trout
  (see page 68)
rocket, spinach and watercress leaves,
  to serve

POTATO LATKES:
750g/1lb 10oz white floury potatoes,
  such as Desiree, peeled
5 tbsp plain flour
1 tsp baking powder
1 tsp salt

2 eggs, lightly beaten
4 tbsp olive oil, for drizzling and frying

BEETROOT RELISH:
400g/14oz uncooked beetroot, washed,
  roots trimmed and quartered
125ml/4fl oz/½ cup crème fraîche
2 tbsp lemon juice
2 tbsp horseradish sauce
1 tbsp chopped dill, for sprinkling
sea salt and freshly ground black pepper

Preheat the oven to 180°C/350°F/Gas 4. Line two baking sheets with a double layer of kitchen paper. To make the beetroot relish, cook the beetroot in a pan of boiling water for 20 minutes until softened but not cooked through. Transfer the beetroot to a roasting tin. Drizzle 1 teaspoon of the olive oil over the beetroot and turn until it is coated, then season with salt and pepper. Roast for 30–35 minutes until tender and the skin is crinkled and slightly caramelized.

While the beetroot is roasting, grate the potatoes over the large holes of a box grater – ideally you want long, thin strands of potato. Transfer the potatoes to a clean kitchen towel or square of muslin and wring out as much liquid as possible.

Mix together the flour, baking powder and salt in large bowl. Season with pepper and add the potato. Stir the potato until evenly coated in the flour mixture, then add the eggs and mix again.

Heat 3 tablespoons of the olive oil in a large, heavy-based frying pan over a medium heat. Take a small handful of the potato mixture, letting the eggy batter drain off a little, and put it into the pan. Flatten slightly with a spatula into a rough-edged 7.5cm/3in round and repeat so you have 3 or 4 latkes in the pan, then fry for 3–4 minutes on each side until golden and crisp. Transfer the latkes to a prepared baking sheet and keep warm in the oven while you cook the remaining latkes. The mixture will make 8 latkes in total.

When the beetroot is cooked, remove it from the oven. Rub off some of the skin if it is loose (you don't need to remove it all) and cut the beetroot into small pieces. Mix together the crème fraîche, lemon juice and horseradish in a bowl. Season, then stir in the beetroot until combined. Sprinkle the dill over the top. Cut the smoked trout into bite-sized pieces and serve with the potato latkes, a good spoonful of the beetroot relish and with rocket, spinach and watercress leaves.

3. Cheese & Dairy

Tomme
Fleurie
D'Alpage
98

BUFFALO MOZZARELLA & SALAMI BRUSCHETTA WITH BASIL OIL

Buffalo mozzarella is perfect here as its fresh, slightly sour, milky flavour and soft texture temper the piquant saltiness of the cured, air-dried salami. The success of this recipe lies almost exclusively with the quality of the ingredients, so choose the best you can afford and you'll be rewarded with great-tasting bruschetta.

SERVES 4   PREPARATION TIME: 20 MINUTES   COOKING TIME: 20 MINUTES

8 thick slices of country-style bread
2 large garlic cloves, halved
250g/9oz buffalo mozzarella cheese, patted dry and sliced
16 thin slices of salami of your choice, outer casing removed
6 large vine-ripened tomatoes, quartered, deseeded and diced

BASIL OIL:
2 large handfuls of basil leaves, plus extra for sprinkling
1 garlic clove, crushed
juice of ½ lemon
6 tbsp extra virgin olive oil, plus extra for brushing
sea salt and freshly ground black pepper

Heat a large griddle pan over a high heat. Griddle the bread, 2 or 3 slices at a time, until toasted and slightly charred in places.

Meanwhile, make the basil oil. Blend together the basil, garlic, lemon juice and olive oil in a mini food processor until combined. Season with salt and pepper and leave to one side.

Rub the cut-side of the garlic over the top of each slice of the toasted bread, then brush with a little of the olive oil. Top with the slices of mozzarella, salami and diced tomatoes. Season with salt and pepper and drizzle the basil oil over the top. Serve at room temperature, sprinkled with basil leaves.

Mozzarella

In Italy, delis and supermarkets proudly display large, open containers of fresh mozzarella in all shapes and sizes, from the smallest bocconcini to the most-prized burrata and mozzarella di bufala. While most mozzarella is now made from cow's milk, it is still possible to buy the traditional buffalo milk alternative. This fresh, unripened cheese is the classic pizza topping, but it's also great in salads such as the classic insalata caprese. Belonging to the same family as mozzarella is scamorza (and the smoked version, scamorza affumicata). It has an unusual pear shape and a slightly firmer, drier texture than mozzarella. Burrata is also worth trying in this recipe. This rich, indulgent cheese has an outer shell of mozzarella with a creamy interior – delicious!

CORNISH BLUE, LARDON & CARAMELIZED APPLE SALAD

The multi-award-winning Cornish Blue is a relatively new cheese, but it is definitely making its mark with cheese aficionados. This young blue cheese goes beautifully with the golden sticky apple slices and the nutty earthiness of the toasted walnuts in this recipe. If you can't find Cornish Blue, French Roquefort or Italian Dolcelatte are more than suitable alternatives.

SERVES 4   PREPARATION TIME: 20 MINUTES   COOKING TIME: 20 MINUTES

70g/2½ oz/scant ½ cup walnut halves
25g/1oz butter
2 firm, crisp apples, peeled, cored and
  sliced into wedges
1 tbsp clear honey
270g/9½ oz bacon lardons
200g/7oz watercress, tough stalks
  removed
150g/5½ oz Cornish Blue cheese, or other
  blue cheese of choice, cut or crumbled
  into bite-sized chunks

DRESSING:
5 tbsp extra virgin olive oil
2 tbsp lemon juice
1 tsp Dijon mustard
sea salt and fresh ground black pepper

Mix together the ingredients for the dressing and season lightly with salt and more generously with pepper, bearing in mind that the lardons and the blue cheese are quite salty.

Toast the walnuts in a large, dry frying pan for 2–3 minutes on each side until they start to colour. Remove from the pan and leave to cool.

Melt the butter in the frying pan. Add the apple wedges and cook for 5 minutes, turning once. Stir in the honey, turn the apples to coat them in the buttery honey sauce and cook for another minute, or until golden. Remove from the pan and leave to one side.

Wipe the pan clean, then add the lardons and cook over a low heat until the fat begins to seep out. Turn the heat up slightly and cook the lardons for 6–8 minutes until golden and crisp. Remove from the pan with a slotted spoon and drain on kitchen paper.

Spoon as much of the dressing over the watercress as needed to coat the leaves. Toss until combined then scatter the walnuts, lardons, Cornish Blue and apples over the top.

Labneh

This Middle Eastern drained yogurt cheese is similar in consistency to a thick cream cheese or curd cheese. Easy to make at home, labneh is the perfect starting point for burgeoning cheesemakers. Do make sure you use good-quality Greek yogurt or thick natural yogurt for the best flavour and texture. Here, walnut-sized balls of labneh are stored in a herb olive oil, but there are many variations, both sweet and savoury, that are worth experimenting with. You'll find some ideas below.

MAKES 16 WALNUT-SIZED BALLS   PREPARATION TIME: 30 MINUTES, PLUS AT LEAST 12 HOURS DRAINING

500ml/17fl oz/2 cups good-quality Greek yogurt or thick natural yogurt
1½ tsp sea salt
4 oregano or marjoram sprigs
4 thyme sprigs
extra virgin olive oil, to cover

Rest a sieve over a medium-sized mixing bowl and line with a piece of muslin or a clean J-cloth.

Mix the yogurt with the salt and spoon it into the cloth-lined sieve. Pull the cloth up around the yogurt and twist the top to make a bundle. Leave the yogurt to drain in the fridge for 12 hours and preferably up to 24 hours; the longer you leave it the firmer the labneh will be. Give the bundle a gentle squeeze every so often to encourage any whey to drain away.

Remove the muslin bundle from the sieve and open it to reveal a smooth, thick soft cheese. The labneh is ready to eat now, or can be formed into balls and stored in olive oil.

To store in olive oil, roll the labneh into 16 small walnut-sized balls. Put the labneh in a large sterilized jar, add the herbs and pour over enough olive oil to cover. Put on the lid and keep in the fridge for up to 1 week.

VARIATIONS
• Add sun-dried tomatoes, chilli or whole spices such as coriander to the jar.
• Roll the balls of labneh in chopped fresh herbs mixed with a little chopped red chilli until coated before putting them in the jar. Try experimenting with ground spices, too.
• Tip the labneh out of the muslin onto a serving plate after draining. Drizzle with good-quality clear honey and scatter a handful of roughly chopped toasted walnuts over the top. Serve with fresh ripe figs or peach slices.

LABNEH & LAMB FLATBREADS WITH MINT SALSA

With the marinade and mint salsa packed with the bold flavours and vibrant colours of North Africa, the balls of labneh add a touch of calm with their soothing, creamy, slightly acidic taste.

**SERVES 4   PREPARATION TIME: 30 MINUTES, PLUS MARINATING
COOKING TIME: 10 MINUTES**

500g/1lb 2oz boneless lamb steaks or
  lamb loin steaks
4 Middle Eastern flatbreads, warmed
2 handfuls of baby spinach leaves
½ recipe quantity Labneh (see page 78)
  or 200g/7oz feta cheese, crumbled
sea salt and freshly ground black pepper

MARINADE:
2 tsp dried mint
2 tsp ground cumin
4 tsp ground coriander
½ tsp chilli powder
3 tbsp olive oil
1 tbsp lemon juice

MINT SALSA:
5 large vine-ripened tomatoes, quartered,
  deseeded and diced
½ small red onion, diced
1 heaped tbsp chopped peppadew
  chillies, drained
1 large handful of mint leaves, roughly
  chopped
2 tbsp extra virgin olive oil
juice of ½ lemon

Mix together all the ingredients for the marinade in a large, shallow non-metallic dish. Add the lamb to the dish and spoon the marinade over until the meat is well coated. Season the lamb with salt and pepper and leave to marinate for 1 hour, covered.

Meanwhile, mix together the ingredients for the mint salsa in a serving bowl. Season with salt and pepper to taste and leave at room temperature until ready to serve.

Heat a large griddle pan over a high heat. Griddle the lamb for 5 minutes or until cooked to your liking, turning once; it should still be pink in the centre. You may need to cook the lamb in batches. Transfer the lamb to a plate, cover with foil and leave to rest for 5 minutes. Cut the lamb into long slices.

To serve, top the warm flatbreads with the spinach and lamb. Crumble the labneh on top and let everyone help themselves to the mint salsa at the table.

CRISPY MANCHEGO WITH CHORIZO-SPIKED RATATOUILLE

The chorizo gives a real kick to this vibrantly coloured ratatouille, similar to the Spanish pisto. The Manchego slices are fried in breadcrumbs to give them a crisp, golden coating.

SERVES 4   PREPARATION TIME: 25 MINUTES   COOKING TIME: 25 MINUTES

50g/1¾oz plain flour
2 eggs, beaten
70g/2½oz/¾ cup fresh breadcrumbs
250g/9oz Manchego cheese, rind removed, cut into 12 fingers
100ml/3½fl oz/generous ⅓ cup vegetable oil

CHORIZO-SPIKED RATATOUILLE:
2 tbsp olive oil
1 large onion, sliced
1 tsp dried oregano

3 garlic cloves, finely chopped
1 red and 1 yellow pepper, deseeded and cut into bite-sized pieces
100g/3½oz cooking chorizo, roughly chopped
6 small courgettes, sliced
4 large vine-ripened tomatoes, deseeded and roughly chopped
1 handful of parsley, leaves chopped
1 handful of basil, leaves torn
50g/1¾oz black olives
sea salt and freshly ground black pepper

First make the chorizo-spiked ratatouille. Heat the olive oil in a large, heavy-based pan and fry the onion for 8 minutes until softened. Add the oregano, garlic, red and yellow peppers, chorizo and courgettes and fry for a further 3–4 minutes, stirring occasionally, until the vegetables soften. Add the tomatoes and cook for 5 minutes until they break down slightly to make a sauce, then stir in the herbs and olives. Season with salt and pepper to taste. Cover the pan with a lid and keep warm while you prepare the Manchego.

Put the flour, eggs and breadcrumbs into three separate shallow bowls. Dip each stick of Manchego into the beaten egg, followed by the flour, then in the egg again and finally the breadcrumbs until coated.

Heat the vegetable oil in a deep frying pan over a medium heat. Cook the bread-crumbed Manchego in three batches for about 1 minute on each side until crisp and golden. Drain on kitchen paper. Serve the ratatouille topped with the crispy Manchego.

Manchego

Manchego is probably Spain's best known cheese. It is produced all over the country, but the true Manchego is made from the milk of the Manchego sheep from the La Mancha region. It has a good depth of flavour with a buttery, nutty taste and a firm, slightly crumbly texture.

BAKED FETA & PRAWNS WITH CHERMOULA

Baking does great things to feta, tempering its saltiness and giving it a much smoother, creamier texture. Serve the feta whole at the table with the baked prawns and let everyone help themselves, peeling and dunking the prawns into the Moroccan chermoula. This fragrant, spicy, herby concoction is traditionally used as a marinade, but it's just as good as a sauce or dip.

SERVES 4   PREPARATION TIME: 25 MINUTES   COOKING TIME: 18 MINUTES

400g/14oz block feta cheese, drained
    and patted dry
4 tbsp extra virgin olive oil
3 oregano sprigs
3 thyme sprigs
½ tsp dried mint
4 garlic cloves, sliced
450g/1lb raw king prawns in their shell
a large pinch of dried chilli flakes
3 tbsp white wine
sea salt and freshly ground black pepper
crusty bread and green salad, to serve

CHERMOULA:
2 handfuls of coriander, leaves chopped
2 handfuls of flat-leaf parsley, leaves
    chopped
2 garlic cloves, finely chopped
1 tsp harissa paste
1 red chilli, deseeded and finely chopped
1 tsp ground cumin
1 tsp ground coriander
juice of 1 large lemon
4 tbsp extra virgin olive oil

Preheat the oven to 200°C/400°F/Gas 6. To make the chermoula, mix together all the ingredients in a bowl and season. Leave to one side to allow the flavours to merge together.

Put a piece of foil large enough to wrap the feta on a large baking tray. Put the feta in the centre of the foil and pour 2 tablespoons of the olive oil over, then top with the oregano, thyme, mint and 1 of the sliced garlic cloves. Season with pepper, bring up the sides of the foil and scrunch the top to make a loose parcel. Bake for 15–18 minutes until softened.

Meanwhile, put the prawns in a large ovenproof dish with the remaining sliced garlic, the chilli flakes, the remaining olive oil and the white wine. Season with salt and bake for 8–10 minutes, basting the prawns occasionally with the juices in the dish until pink and cooked through.

Transfer the feta to a plate and serve in slices with the prawns and their cooking juices and a good spoonful of the chermoula. Serve with crusty bread and a green salad.

TWICE-BAKED CHEESE SOUFFLÉS WITH PEAR & RED LEAF SALAD

These soufflés can be made the day before serving them and the best thing about baking them twice is you don't need to worry whether they will rise; magically, they rise again when baked for the second time. Be warned – they are rich and indulgent, but quite delectable!

**SERVES 4   PREPARATION TIME: 30 MINUTES, PLUS INFUSING AND COOLING
COOKING TIME: 45 MINUTES**

200ml/7fl oz/scant 1 cup whole milk
1 bay leaf
1 large garlic clove, peeled and halved
50g/1¾oz butter
40g/1½oz/⅓ cup plain flour
2 tsp Dijon mustard
100g/3½oz mature Cheddar cheese, grated
50g/1¾oz aged Gruyère cheese, grated
3 eggs, separated
4 tbsp double cream

PEAR AND RED LEAF SALAD:
8 red leaf lettuce leaves, torn
50g/1¾oz red cabbage, shredded
2 crisp but ripe pears, cored and sliced lengthways, tossed in a little lemon juice
2 tbsp extra virgin olive oil
1 tbsp lemon juice
2 tbsp snipped chives
sea salt and freshly ground black pepper

Warm the milk in a small pan with the bay leaf and garlic. Turn off the heat and leave the milk to infuse for 30 minutes. Reheat just before using. Preheat the oven to 200°C/400°F/Gas 6 and heat a large baking tray. Melt the butter in a medium-sized pan and use a little to grease four 175ml/5½fl oz/⅔ cup ramekins.

Whisk the remaining melted butter with the flour over a medium heat and cook the roux for 1 minute, stirring. Remove the bay leaf and garlic from the warm milk and gradually stir it into the roux. Bring to the boil, then turn the heat down and simmer for 5 minutes, stirring continuously until thick and smooth.

Pour the white sauce into a bowl and stir in the mustard, Cheddar and 2 tablespoons of the Gruyère. Beat in the egg yolks, one at a time. In a separate large bowl, whisk the egg whites until they form stiff peaks. Using a metal spoon, fold the egg whites into the cheese mixture in three batches; spoon this into the ramekins.

Put the ramekins on the heated baking tray and bake for 18–20 minutes until risen. Leave to cool, run a knife around the edge of the soufflés and carefully turn them out. Chill until ready to serve.

Heat the oven to 220°C/425°F/Gas 7. Put the soufflés on a baking tray, then spoon 1 tablespoon of the cream and the remaining Gruyère over each one. Bake for 10–12 minutes until risen and the cheese has melted.

Meanwhile, to make the salad, put the lettuce, red cabbage and pears in a serving bowl. Whisk together the olive oil and lemon juice, season with salt and pepper and spoon the dressing over the salad. Toss until combined and scatter the chives over the top. Serve the soufflés with the salad.

HALLOUMI, FIG & ALMOND SALAD

The sweet succulence of the fig makes it a great match for the salty, firm halloumi cheese in this salad. When buying figs, look for ripe fruits that yield slightly when pressed lightly as these will have the best flavour. Since figs don't ripen after picking, you want to avoid fruit that is too firm as it will be lacking in sweetness. Plan to make this salad just before serving, as halloumi is at its best when still warm and softened by the heat.

SERVES 4   PREPARATION TIME: 15 MINUTES   COOKING TIME: 10 MINUTES

75g/2½ oz/scant ½ cup blanched almonds
2 handfuls of rocket leaves
2 handfuls of pea shoots
6 figs, quartered
1 tbsp olive oil
250g/9oz halloumi cheese, patted dry
   and cubed
5 mint sprigs, leaves torn

DRESSING:
4 tbsp extra virgin olive oil
1 tbsp red wine vinegar
1 tsp clear honey
½ tsp Dijon mustard
sea salt and freshly ground black pepper

Mix together all the ingredients for the dressing and season with salt and pepper.

Toast the almonds in a large, dry frying pan over a medium heat for about 5 minutes, turning once, until they are lightly browned. Leave to cool.

Meanwhile, put the rocket, pea shoots and figs on a large serving bowl. Scatter the almonds over the salad.

Heat the oil in the frying pan and cook the halloumi for about 5 minutes, turning occasionally, until softened and just golden in places. Scatter the halloumi over the salad. Spoon as much of the dressing over the top as required then toss until everything is coated and combined. Sprinkle the mint over before serving.

Halloumi Cheese

A traditional ewe's and goat's milk cheese from Cyprus, halloumi has a high melting point so it holds its shape when heated. You don't want to heat it for too long, though, as it can become tough and rubbery – it needs just long enough to soften it and to give a slightly golden crust. It's definitely a cheese that is best served warm. Always pat halloumi dry with kitchen paper before cooking – this means that it will become crisp and golden rather than soggy and water-logged.

Home-made Buttermilk

At first I wasn't sure about including this recipe for buttermilk because it's so very simple. But I decided to put it in since it can be difficult to find in shops and it makes a versatile and useful addition to a cook's repertoire. Once a by-product of butter-making, buttermilk was the liquid left in the churn after butter was made. It has a slightly sour, acidic taste and is usually used in baking. Scones, pancakes, soda bread and cakes all benefit from the addition of buttermilk. So, too, does a marinade for meat or poultry (see page 89), since it improves the texture of meat and makes it incredibly tender. This recipe will result in a rich buttermilk that's equivalent to traditional versions, but you could replace the whole milk with low-fat milk and omit the cream.

MAKES 325ML/11FL OZ/SCANT 1⅓ CUPS   PREPARATION TIME: 5 MINUTES, PLUS STANDING

300ml/10½ fl oz/scant 1¼ cups whole milk
4 tsp lemon juice or white vinegar
1 tbsp double cream (optional)

Put the milk in a jug and stir in the lemon juice. Leave to stand at room temperature for about 20 minutes until it starts to curdle. Stir in the cream, if using.

Stir well before use, then use as instructed in your recipe. It will keep, covered, in the fridge for up to 2 days.

BUTTERMILK ROAST CHICKEN

Buttermilk makes a surprisingly good marinade, because it relaxes the proteins in the meat, keeping it tender and moist. For the best results, leave the chicken to marinate overnight.

**SERVES 4   PREPARATION TIME: 15 MINUTES, PLUS MARINATING AND RESTING
   COOKING TIME: 1 HOUR 10 MINUTES**

¾ recipe quantity Home-made Buttermilk
   (see page 86)
1 tbsp sea salt
1 tbsp honey
1 tbsp Dijon mustard
1 tsp paprika, plus extra for sprinkling

4 garlic cloves, halved lengthways
1.5kg/3lb 5oz chicken
1 tsp olive oil
freshly ground black pepper
roast new potatoes, rocket salad and
   Mayonnaise (see page 126), to serve

Mix together the buttermilk, salt, honey, mustard, paprika and garlic in a bowl, and season with pepper. Put the chicken in a large, strong freezer bag with a ziplock fastener. Pour the marinade into the bag, then seal. Turn the chicken to coat it in the marinade and put the bag in a roasting tin. Leave to marinate in the fridge for up to 24 hours. Turn the chicken occasionally to ensure all parts of the bird get a good coating of the marinade.

Preheat the oven to 190°/375°F/Gas 5. Remove the chicken from the bag and put it in a foil-lined roasting tin. Discard the marinade. Drizzle the oil over and season with more paprika, salt and pepper. Roast for 1 hour 10 minutes or until cooked through, occasionally basting the chicken. Cover the chicken with foil to keep it warm and leave to rest for 15 minutes. Serve with roasted new potatoes, rocket salad and a spoonful of mayonnaise.

SLOW-COOKED PORK IN MILK

Inspired by the Italian dish arista al latte, the pork steaks here are slow-cooked in milk and infused with lemon, oregano and garlic. The milk keeps the meat moist and has a tenderizing effect, and it cooks down to a light, fragrant sauce. The pork is delicious served with crisp roast potatoes, steamed courgettes and long-stem broccoli.

SERVES 4   PREPARATION TIME: 20 MINUTES   COOKING TIME: 2 HOURS 5 MINUTES

4 rindless pork shoulder steaks, about 225g/8oz each
1 tbsp olive oil
25g/1oz butter
3 garlic cloves, sliced
5 oregano sprigs, plus 1 tbsp leaves for sprinkling
600ml/21fl oz/scant 2½ cups whole milk
4 strips of pared lemon zest
2 bay leaves
sea salt and freshly ground black pepper
roast potatoes, green vegetables and lemon wedges, to serve

Season both sides of each pork steak. Heat the oil in a large casserole and sear the pork over a medium-high heat in two batches until browned on both sides. Remove the pork from the casserole and leave to one side.

Turn the heat down slightly, melt the butter and add the garlic and oregano sprigs. Return the pork to the casserole, pour the milk over and tuck the lemon zest and bay leaves between the steaks.

Bring the milk in the casserole to the boil, then turn the heat down to very low and simmer the pork, part-covered, for 45 minutes. Turn the steaks in the milk every 20 minutes. The liquid should simmer very gently all the time to allow the milk to reduce gradually and the pork to cook slowly.

Remove the lid and continue to simmer the pork for a further 45 minutes. The milk will have curdled, but this is perfectly normal. Remove the pork using a spatula and leave it to rest, covered in foil, for 5 minutes.

Season the sauce, bring to the boil, then allow to gently bubble away for 5 minutes until reduced by a third and almost caramel in colour. Strain and discard the solids.

Serve the pork with the sauce spooned over the top, scattered with extra oregano and with roast potatoes, green vegetables and lemon wedges for squeezing over.

TARTIFLETTE

Winter food at its best, this comforting potato, bacon and cheese gratin originates from the Haute-Savoie region of France. It is traditionally made with Reblochon, a cow's milk cheese with a slightly nutty flavour, soft interior and pinkish-brown rind. Serve it with charcuterie, pickled onions and gherkins.

**SERVES 4 (SERVES 6 AS A SIDE DISH)   PREPARATION TIME: 15 MINUTES
COOKING TIME: 50 MINUTES**

1kg/2lb 4oz waxy potatoes, such as
   Charlotte
1 tsp olive oil
200g/7oz bacon lardons
1 onion, roughly chopped
3 garlic cloves, roughly chopped
115ml/3¾fl oz/scant ½ cup dry
   white wine

200ml/7fl oz/scant 1 cup double cream
about 350g/12oz Reblochon cheese, rind
   removed and sliced
sea salt and freshly ground black pepper
charcuterie, pickled onions and gherkins,
   to serve

Preheat the oven to 200°C/400°F/Gas 6. Cook the potatoes in a pan of boiling salted water for 10–15 minutes until tender. Drain and leave to one side until cool enough to handle.

Meanwhile, put the olive oil and lardons in a dry non-stick frying pan and heat over a low heat until the fat starts to seep out of the lardons. Turn the heat up to medium, add the onion and cook for 5–6 minutes until the onion has softened and the lardons are crisp. Add the garlic and cook for another minute.

Pour in the wine and stir well to remove any sticky brown bits at the bottom of the pan, then continue to cook until most of the wine has evaporated.

Slice the potatoes and gently mix with the lardon mixture in an ovenproof dish. Pour the cream over the top and season with pepper (you are unlikely to need more salt). Lay the Reblochon on top and bake for 20 minutes until the cheese has melted and is golden in places. Serve with charcuterie, pickled onions and gherkins.

Washed-Rind Cheese

Reblochon is the traditional cheese for tartiflette, but if you can't get hold of it you could try another washed-rind cheese such as Epoisses, Taleggio or Fontina, which all have a similar sweet, nutty, earthy flavour and are good to cook with as they have excellent melting qualities. I prefer to remove the hard rind before use, but this is a personal choice.

STEAK WITH DOLCELATTE SAUCE & BALSAMIC TOMATOES

The blue-veined Dolcelatte cheese melts down into a rich, creamy, slightly sweet sauce. You will need to take the steak out of the fridge an hour before you intend to cook it and bring it up to room temperature, and pat it dry to remove any excess moisture. The sauce is best served in small amounts, rather than being poured over and smothering the meat.

SERVES 4   PREPARATION TIME: 20 MINUTES   COOKING TIME: 20 MINUTES

4 fillet steaks, about 200g/7oz each, at
   room temperature and patted dry
sea salt and freshly ground black pepper
crusty bread, to serve

BALSAMIC TOMATOES:
4 tbsp olive oil
350g/12oz cherry tomatoes, halved
4 thyme sprigs, leaves removed
2 tbsp balsamic vinegar

DOLCELATTE SAUCE:
4 tbsp dry white wine
150g/5½ oz Dolcelatte cheese, rind
   removed and cut into pieces
140ml/4¾ fl oz/generous ½ cup crème
   fraîche

To make the balsamic tomatoes, heat 3 tablespoons of the olive oil in a frying pan over a medium-low heat. Add the tomatoes and half of the thyme, then cook for 1 minute. Turn the tomatoes over and pour in the balsamic vinegar. Cook for another 2 minutes until the balsamic vinegar reduces and the tomatoes start to caramelize. Season with salt and pepper, then leave to one side.

Rub the steaks with a little olive oil, then season each side with salt and pepper.

Heat a large griddle or frying pan over a high heat. Add the steaks, turn the heat down to medium and cook for about 5–6 minutes – you will probably have to cook them in two batches – turning them twice and occasionally pressing the meat down into the pan. The steaks should be seared on the outside but medium-rare in the centre. Transfer the steaks to a warm plate and leave to rest, covered with foil, for 5 minutes.

To make the Dolcelatte sauce, add the wine to the pan with the juices from the steaks. Stir to release any bits stuck to the bottom of the pan and simmer until reduced by half. Pour this into a saucepan if you are using a griddle pan and add the Dolcelatte and crème fraîche. Heat through, stirring, until the cheese has melted, then season with pepper.

Top each steak with a generous spoonful of the Dolcelatte sauce and serve with the tomatoes, sprinkled with the remaining thyme, and crusty bread.

Home-made Crème Fraîche

Velvety, slightly nutty and with a gentle tang, crème fraîche lends a smooth, mellow creaminess to savoury sauces, or a spoonful curbs the sweetness of a cake or dessert. Crème fraîche is similar to soured cream, but has a thicker texture and is not quite as tangy. It is more stable, too, resisting curdling and separation when heated, which makes it ideal in cooking. While crème fraîche is widely available, there's nothing like making your own and it takes very little effort.

MAKES 300ML/10½FL OZ/SCANT 1¼ CUPS   PREPARATION TIME: 10 MINUTES, PLUS UP TO 24 HOURS STANDING

300ml/10½ fl oz/scant 1¼ cups double cream
2 tbsp buttermilk

Pour the cream into a saucepan and gently warm it over a medium-low heat until it reaches 40°C/105°F. Remove from the heat and pour it into a sterilized glass jar. Stir in the buttermilk until combined, then cover with cling film or baking paper and secure with an elastic band.

Put the jar in a warm, draught-free place and leave to thicken – this can take anything from 12 to 24 hours. Once thickened, stir well, then cover with a lid and chill. The crème fraîche is ready to eat but will continue to thicken. Store in the fridge for up to 2 weeks.

SALMON, LEEK & **CRÈME FRAÎCHE** PLAIT

This is an ideal summery alternative to a Sunday roast. The fillet of salmon is encased in layer of creamy leeks and puff pastry, then baked until flaky and golden. Go for a mid-cut salmon fillet – it's likely to be of an even thickness and will ensure the fish cooks evenly.

SERVES 6   PREPARATION TIME: 30 MINUTES   COOKING TIME: 45 MINUTES

butter, for greasing
2 leeks, finely chopped
1 large handful of watercress, roughly
    chopped
½ recipe quantity Home-made Crème
    Fraîche (see page 94), about
    150ml/5fl oz/scant ⅔ cup
680g/1lb 8oz salmon fillet, skin removed
375g/13oz ready-rolled puff pastry

flour, for dusting
1 egg yolk, lightly beaten
sea salt and freshly ground black pepper
new potatoes and green beans, to serve

CHIVE AND LEMON MAYONNAISE:
100g/3½ oz Mayonnaise (see page 126)
juice of ½ lemon
1 tbsp snipped chives

Preheat the oven to 200°C/400°F/Gas 6 and lightly grease a large baking tray with butter.

Steam the leeks for 5 minutes until tender. Leave until cool enough to handle, then squeeze out as much water as possible, using your hands. This will prevent the pastry becoming soggy during baking. Put the leeks in a mixing bowl and stir in the watercress and crème fraîche. Season with salt and pepper.

Using a pair of tweezers, remove any bones in the salmon and pat the fillet dry with kitchen paper.

Roll out the pastry slightly on a lightly floured work surface into a large rectangle the same length as the salmon and just over double the width. Lay the salmon lengthways down the centre of the pastry, then spoon the leek mixture over the top in an even layer.

Make diagonal cuts into the pastry down both sides of the salmon to make even-sized strips; if you cut away the corners, this makes the pastry easier to plait. Fold each end of the pastry over the filling. Begin to plait, taking one of the strips and folding it over the filling, then take one from the other side and fold that over. Continue until you have plaited the pastry all the way down to make a long log shape.

Using two spatulas, carefully transfer the plait to the prepared baking tray. Brush the pastry with the egg yolk. Bake the plait for 35–40 minutes until golden and the pastry is cooked through.

Meanwhile, mix together the mayonnaise and lemon juice. Add 1 tablespoon water to loosen the mixture, then scatter the chives over the top. Serve the salmon plait in slices with a spoonful of the mayonnaise, new potatoes and green beans.

SMOKED HADDOCK WITH TALEGGIO SAUCE

The northern Italian cheese Taleggio (see page 91), with its semi-soft texture and slightly fruity flavour, melts down into a wonderfully rich and creamy sauce with a robust aroma. Served with smoked haddock and a poached egg, this is a heart-warming combination.

SERVES 4   PREPARATION TIME: 15 MINUTES   COOKING TIME: 20 MINUTES

4 undyed thick smoked haddock fillets, about 175g/6oz each
1 tsp olive oil
½ lemon, cut into 4 slices
4 large eggs
240ml/8fl oz/scant 1 cup dry white wine
175g/6oz Taleggio cheese, rind removed and cut into pieces

1 tsp cornflour, mixed with 1 tsp whole milk
1 tbsp double cream
250g/9oz Swiss chard or spinach
freshly ground black pepper
crusty bread, to serve

Preheat the oven to 190°C/375°F/Gas 5. Put a piece of foil large enough to make a parcel for the haddock fillets on a baking tray and lightly grease with the olive oil. Put the haddock on the foil, season with pepper and put a slice of lemon on top of each. Bring up the sides of the foil and scrunch the top to make a loose parcel. Bake for 15–20 minutes, depending on the thickness of the fillets, until opaque.

Meanwhile, poach the eggs 5 minutes after putting the haddock in the oven. Put a wide, deep frying pan on the hob and fill with about 2.5cm/1in just-boiled water from a kettle. Keep the heat low, break the eggs, one at a time, into a cup, then slip them into the just simmering water. Repeat so you are cooking all 4 eggs at the same time. Cook the eggs for 1 minute, then turn the heat off and let the eggs sit in the hot water for 10 minutes or until the white is cooked and the yolk is still slightly runny.

To make the Taleggio sauce, pour the wine into a small pan and bring to the boil. Turn the heat down to medium-low and let the wine bubble away until reduced by a third and there is no aroma of alcohol.

Stir in the Taleggio and, when melted, add the cornflour mixture. Cook for about 3 minutes, stirring until thickened slightly and the sauce coats the back of a spoon. Stir in the double cream, cover with a lid and leave to one side.

Steam the chard or spinach for 3 minutes, or until wilted.

To serve, divide the chard or spinach into four bowls. Remove the haddock from its foil parcel and put on top. Using a slotted spoon, lift out the eggs, one at a time, and then let the egg rest on a few sheets of kitchen paper, which will absorb any excess water. Put an egg on each fish fillet and spoon the sauce over. Season with pepper before serving with crusty bread.

HERB RICOTTA CHEESECAKE WITH ROASTED TOMATO PESTO

The delicate freshness of ricotta cheese is the perfect foundation for this light, savoury cheesecake. Boosted by the rich, earthy flavour of the Parmesan and a smattering of fresh herbs, the cheesecake is topped with a vibrant tomato pesto. Look for the most flavoursome tomatoes you can find and a good fruity olive oil.

SERVES 6–8   PREPARATION TIME: 25 MINUTES   COOKING TIME: 1 HOUR

750g/1lb 10oz/3 cups ricotta cheese
85g/3oz Parmesan cheese, finely grated
3 large eggs, separated
1 handful of basil, leaves torn, plus whole leaves for sprinkling
1 handful of oregano, leaves roughly chopped
2 tbsp snipped chives
1 tsp sea salt
freshly ground black pepper
crisp green salad, to serve

ROASTED TOMATO PESTO:
6 large vine-ripened tomatoes, quartered and deseeded
80ml/2½ fl oz/⅓ cup extra virgin olive oil, plus extra for greasing
70g/2½ oz drained sun-blush tomatoes in oil, roughly chopped
1 garlic clove, crushed
4 tbsp blanched almonds, toasted and roughly chopped

Preheat the oven to 180°C/350°F/Gas 4 and lightly oil a 20cm/8in loose-bottomed cake tin.

Put the ricotta, Parmesan and egg yolks in a food processor and blend until smooth and creamy. Transfer the ricotta mixture to a large mixing bowl and stir in the basil, oregano, chives and salt, then season with plenty of freshly ground pepper.

Whisk the egg whites in a separate bowl until they form stiff peaks. Using a metal spoon, gently fold the egg whites into the ricotta mixture and mix until combined. Spoon the mixture into the prepared tin and smooth with a palette knife. Put the tin on a baking sheet and bake for about 1 hour until risen, set and light golden.

Meanwhile, make the roasted tomato pesto. Halfway through the cheesecake cooking time, put the tomatoes in a roasting tin with 2 tablespoons of the oil, season, then turn the tomatoes in the oil. Put them in the top half of the oven with the cheesecake and roast for 30 minutes until softened and slightly wrinkly.

Remove the tomatoes and cheesecake and leave the latter to cool slightly while you make the pesto. Put the roasted tomatoes, sun-blush tomatoes, garlic, 2 tablespoons of the nuts and the remaining oil in a food processor and process to a coarse paste; season to taste with salt and pepper. Spoon the pesto into a bowl and add a splash more oil if it seems too dry.

Run a knife around the edge of the cheesecake and remove it from the tin. Serve cut into wedges with the basil leaves and remaining chopped nuts scattered over the top, and with the tomato pesto and salad.

MUSHROOM, CAMEMBERT & MEMBRILLO WELLINGTONS

The intensely fruity, ruby-red membrillo, or Spanish quince paste or "cheese", is perfect combined with melting Camembert in these individual baked filo pastry parcels. Use a Camembert that is just ripe so that it melts but doesn't run away during baking.

SERVES 4   PREPARATION TIME: 15 MINUTES   COOKING TIME: 35 MINUTES

olive oil, for greasing and brushing
4 large portobello or field mushrooms, about 250g/9oz total weight
2 x 150g/5½ oz small Camembert cheeses
4 tbsp membrillo

6 sheets of filo pastry, each about 48 x 25cm/19 x 10in
40g/1½ oz butter, melted
sea salt and freshly ground black pepper
new potatoes and green salad, to serve

Preheat the oven to 190°C/375°F/Gas 5 and lightly oil a large baking tray. Brush both sides of each mushroom with olive oil and put them cap-side down on a plate. Season with salt and pepper. Using a sharp knife, slice the rind off the top and the bottom of the Camembert; you can leave the rind around the sides. Cut each Camembert in half crossways to give 4 pieces.

Put a piece of Camembert on top of each mushroom and top with a tablespoonful of the membrillo. Leave to one side.

Cut each sheet of filo in half vertically. Place 3 halves of filo on top of one another, brushing each layer with a little melted butter. Keep the remaining filo covered with a damp kitchen towel to prevent it drying out. Sit the stuffed mushroom in the centre and draw up the corners of the filo to meet in the middle and make a parcel. Twist the top of the filo to seal and brush the parcel with more butter. Repeat with the remaining stuffed mushrooms and filo.

Place the mushroom Wellingtons on the prepared baking tray. Bake for 25–35 minutes until the filo is golden and crisp. Leave to cool slightly to allow the Camembert to firm up before serving with potatoes and salad.

Membrillo

Membrillo has the texture of a firm fruit jelly with a slight graininess and a sweet, floral taste. Traditionally served with Manchego cheese, it is also delicious cut into cubes and offered as a sweetmeat. It can also be used as a glaze or in gravies, and works especially well with fatty meats such as pork or lamb. Although membrillo is the Spanish word for quince, very similar products are made in other countries such as Britain, which has a long history of making fruit cheese.

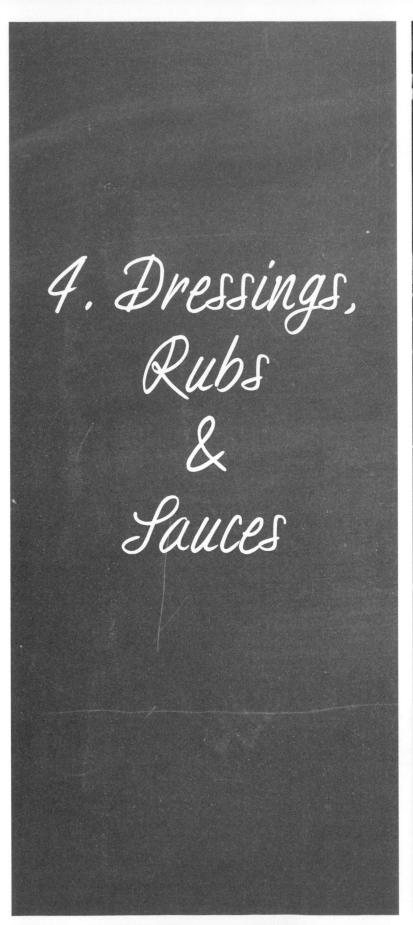

4. Dressings, Rubs & Sauces

DUCK & MANGO SALAD WITH CITRUS DRESSING

Duck and orange are natural partners, with the sour-sweet of the citrus dressing cutting through the rich fattiness of the poultry. This substantial meat salad looks stunning and has just the right balance of flavours and textures.

SERVES 4   PREPARATION TIME: 15 MINUTES   COOKING TIME: 18 MINUTES

4 duck breasts, with skin on, about
175g/6oz each
125g/4½ oz baby spinach leaves
1 red onion, cut into thin rings
1 small mango, peeled and thinly sliced
1 bunch of radishes, sliced into rounds
200g/7oz tinned cannellini beans,
drained and rinsed
1 handful of coriander leaves, torn

CITRUS DRESSING:
3 tbsp extra virgin olive oil
1 tsp balsamic vinegar
juice of ½ large orange
½ orange, peeled and flesh chopped
1 red chilli, deseeded and diced
sea salt and freshly ground black pepper

Preheat the oven to 200°C/400°F/Gas 6 and heat a large baking tray. Put the duck, skin-side down, in a large, dry, non-stick frying pan. Cook over a medium heat for 10 minutes until the fat begins to run and the skin is golden and crisp. Transfer the duck to the preheated baking tray, skin-side up, and roast for 8 minutes until cooked and slightly pink in the centre. Leave to rest, covered with foil, for 5 minutes.

Meanwhile, put the spinach leaves on a large serving plate. Top with the red onion, mango, radishes and beans.

To make the dressing, whisk together the olive oil, vinegar and orange juice in a bowl until combined. Stir in the orange flesh and chilli and season with salt and pepper to taste.

Cut the duck breasts into slices on the diagonal, then put on top of the salad. Spoon the dressing over the top and scatter with the coriander. Serve while the duck is still warm.

SALAD OF SMOKED VENISON, ARTICHOKES & QUAIL'S EGGS WITH WALNUT OIL DRESSING

A sophisticated, impressive salad that is full of flavour: the walnut oil lends a nutty earthiness to the dressing, which complements the richness of the smoked venison.

SERVES 4   PREPARATION TIME: 10 MINUTES   COOKING TIME: 3 MINUTES

12 quail's eggs
225g/8oz mixed salad leaves, to include
   red lettuce
125g/4½ oz tinned or bottled artichoke
   hearts in oil, drained and halved or
   quartered if large
150g/5½ oz sliced cooked smoked
   venison, cut into strips
slices of walnut bread, to serve

WALNUT OIL DRESSING:
5 tbsp walnut oil
1 tbsp extra virgin olive oil
2 tbsp lemon juice
sea salt and freshly ground black pepper

Mix together the ingredients for the dressing until combined, season with salt and pepper to taste, then leave to one side. Put the quail's eggs in a pan, cover with just-boiled water and return to a gentle boil for 2½ minutes. Drain the eggs, cool under cold running water and peel. Halve the eggs and leave to one side.

Put the salad leaves on a serving plate. Top with the artichoke hearts, venison and quail's eggs and spoon enough of the dressing over to coat (you will have some of the dressing left over). Toss lightly before serving immediately with walnut bread.

Smoky Red Pepper Ketchup

Grilling the peppers gives them a delicious smokiness and adds an extra dimension to this ketchup. If making your own ketchup sounds a bit of a faff, this is really worth the effort, as everyone will love it – it also makes a nice change to the tomato variety. It can be used immediately, but store in the fridge after opening and use within 2 months.

MAKES ABOUT 2 X 300G/10½OZ JARS   PREPARATION TIME: 25 MINUTES
COOKING TIME: 1½ HOURS

6 red peppers
2 onions, chopped
2 apples, peeled, cored and chopped
2 celery sticks, sliced
100ml/3½fl oz/generous ⅓ cup cider vinegar
4 thyme sprigs, leaves removed
100g/3½oz/½ cup soft light brown sugar
4 cloves
2 tsp ground allspice
½ tsp ground cinnamon
½ tsp sea salt
a few drops of Tabasco sauce, to taste (optional)
freshly ground black pepper

Preheat the grill to the highest setting. Grill the peppers for 30 minutes, turning them occasionally, until softened and blackened in places. Put the peppers in two plastic bags and leave for 5 minutes (this will make the skins easier to remove). Over a plate to capture any juices, peel and deseed the peppers, then roughly chop them. Strain any juices into a large, non-reactive pan and discard the solids.

Process the onions, apples and celery in a food processor until finely chopped, then tip into the pan. Process the peppers to a coarse purée and add to the pan with 2 tablespoons of the cider vinegar, 100ml/3½fl oz/generous ⅓ cup water and the thyme leaves.

Bring to the boil, then turn the heat down to low, cover and simmer for 30 minutes until the fruit and vegetables have softened. Pass the mixture in batches through a mouli or sieve to a purée.

Return the purée to the cleaned pan and add the remaining vinegar, sugar, cloves, allspice, cinnamon and salt. Season with pepper and bring to the boil, then turn the heat down to low and simmer for another 25–30 minutes until reduced and thickened to a ketchup consistency; stir regularly to prevent it catching on the bottom of the pan. Add a few drops of Tabasco, if you like a little heat.

Pour into your sterilized jars or bottles and seal. The ketchup is ready to use immediately but will keep for up to 2 months unopened and stored in a cool, dark place.

BARBECUE **SMOKY RED PEPPER** PORK WITH COURGETTE TZATZIKI

A few spoonfuls of the Smoky Red Pepper Ketchup on page 106 gives great depth of flavour to this barbecue sauce. A great favourite with kids, something to do with its sweet stickiness no doubt, barbecue sauce is so easy to make at home – all you need is a handful of store-cupboard ingredients to make this condiment-cum-marinade.

**SERVES 4   PREPARATION TIME: 20 MINUTES, PLUS MARINATING
COOKING TIME: 8 MINUTES**

4 pork steaks, about 175g/6oz each,
  fat trimmed
4 Mediterranean or Middle Eastern
  flatbreads, warmed
100g/3½ oz chargrilled red peppers,
  drained and cut into strips
1 red chilli, deseeded and thinly sliced
2 tbsp chopped coriander leaves

BARBECUE SAUCE:
4 tbsp Smoky Red Pepper Ketchup
  (see page 106) or regular tomato
  ketchup

2 tbsp balsamic vinegar
2 tbsp clear honey
1 tbsp dark soy sauce
2 tsp olive oil

COURGETTE TZATZIKI:
150ml/5fl oz/scant ⅔ cup natural yogurt
4 tbsp lemon juice
1 garlic clove, crushed
1 courgette, coarsely grated
sea salt and freshly ground black pepper

Mix together all the ingredients for the barbecue sauce. Put the pork in a non-metallic dish and spoon the barbecue sauce over until both sides of the meat are coated. Leave the meat to marinate, covered, for 1 hour in the fridge.

Preheat the grill to high and line the grill pan with foil. Grill the pork for 4 minutes on each side or until cooked to your liking. (If you have a combined grill/oven, you could warm the flatbreads at the same time and then wrap them in foil to keep them warm.) Cover the pork with foil and leave to rest for 5 minutes.

Meanwhile, mix together the ingredients for the courgette tzatziki and season to taste with salt and pepper. Leave to one side until ready to serve.

To serve, slice the pork into strips and put on top of the warmed flatbreads; pour over any juices left in the foil after resting. Top with the red pepper, the tzatziki, chilli and coriander before serving.

Thai Lemongrass & Chilli Oil

Flavoured oils are a real asset to the store cupboard and are a simple way of adding an instant burst of flavour with very little effort. Herbs and spices are the most obvious flavourings, but you could also add garlic, dried mushrooms, lemon zest or shallots, among many other things. If you have an abundance of fresh herbs, one of the simplest ways to preserve them is in oil (or vinegar), but they are best made in relatively small quantities – since they contain fresh ingredients and do deteriorate with time. It's best to use organic flavourings and make sure they are completely dry before adding them to the oil. This flavoured oil captures many of the flavours of Thai cooking – just add a splash to dressings, Asian soups, curries, noodle and rice dishes.

MAKES 350ML/12FL OZ/SCANT 1½ CUPS   PREPARATION TIME: 10 MINUTES, PLUS COOLING AND 3 DAYS INFUSING   COOKING TIME: 5 MINUTES

350ml/12floz/scant 1½ cups light olive oil, plus extra if needed
½ tsp dried chilli flakes
2 red chillies, halved or quartered
2 lemongrass stalks, outer layers removed and bruised
4 kaffir lime leaves
1 tsp rock salt
2 long Thai basil sprigs

Pour the olive oil into a small saucepan and add the chilli flakes, chillies, lemongrass and lime leaves. Heat the oil for 3 minutes over a medium-low heat. Heating the oil encourages the flavours to infuse efficiently and quickly. Stir in the salt (this will help to keep the oil clear) and leave the oil to cool.

Insert the basil sprigs into a 400ml/14fl oz/generous 1½ cups sterilized bottle. Using tongs, take the lemongrass, fresh chillies and lime leaves out of the oil and put them in the bottle. Using a funnel, pour the oil and chilli flakes into the bottle until everything is completely covered. It is important the oil covers the flavourings – if it doesn't, top up with a little extra oil.

Put the lid on and leave the oil and flavourings to infuse for 3 days, turning the bottle occasionally, then transfer to the fridge and use within 2 weeks.

BEEF CARPACCIO SALAD WITH **THAI LEMONGRASS & CHILLI OIL** DRESSING

Sweet, sour, salty and hot – this fragrant Thai dressing ticks all the right boxes, and rather than masking the earthy flavours of the raw beef, it lifts and complements them. It's a good idea to put the beef in the freezer first to firm up as this will make it so much easier to slice thinly and the other tip is to use a long-bladed, very sharp knife. Choose a thick piece of beef, preferably a centre cut, to allow you to cut slices of a decent size.

SERVES 4   PREPARATION TIME: 15 MINUTES, PLUS FREEZING

200g/7oz piece good-quality sirloin steak
2 handfuls of baby spinach leaves
1 carrot, thinly sliced into thin strips
5cm/2in piece cucumber, quartered
  lengthways, deseeded and cut into
  thin strips
1 small red pepper, deseeded and cut
  into thin strips
¼ small red onion, very thinly sliced
1 small handful of basil, leaves roughly
  torn
1 small handful of coriander, leaves
  roughly chopped

DRESSING:
3 tbsp Thai Lemongrass & Chilli Oil
  (see page 108)
2 tbsp fish sauce
juice of 1 lime
1 tsp caster sugar
sea salt and freshly ground black pepper

Put the steak in the freezer for 30 minutes to firm it up and make it easier to slice.

Meanwhile, mix together all the ingredients for the dressing and season to taste with salt and pepper. Leave to one side.

Divide the spinach onto four plates and top with the carrot, cucumber and red pepper. Spoon enough of the dressing over to coat and toss lightly until combined.

Remove the steak from the freezer and, using a very sharp, long-bladed knife, cut into very thin, elegant slices. Put the cut slices on a plate and cover with cling film to prevent them discolouring as you slice the steak. If you put a layer of cling film between the layers, you'll be able to separate the steak more easily.

Put the steak on top of each serving of salad, season with salt and pepper and scatter the red onion and herbs over the top. Spoon more of the dressing over, to taste, and serve straight away.

KING PRAWN FRITTERS WITH SWEET CHILLI JAM

A great combination of sweet and sticky, this fiery chilli jam can be served as a dip, stirred into oriental sauces or turned into a marinade for meat, poultry and seafood. It's also perfect with these Asian prawn fritters.

**SERVES 4 (CHILLI JAM MAKES 2 X 200G/7OZ JARS)   PREPARATION TIME: 30 MINUTES
COOKING TIME: 35 MINUTES**

350g/12oz raw, peeled, large king
   prawns
2 courgettes, coarsely grated
1 red chilli, deseeded and finely
   chopped
5 tbsp plain flour, plus extra for dusting
1 tsp baking powder
2 tsp ground coriander
½ tsp turmeric
2 spring onions, finely chopped
2 tbsp chopped coriander leaves
1 tsp salt
2 eggs, beaten
groundnut oil, for frying
freshly ground black pepper

shredded Little Gem lettuce leaves,
   shredded spring onions and lime
   wedges, to serve

SWEET CHILLI JAM:
4cm/1½ in piece of fresh root ginger,
   peeled and finely chopped
3 garlic cloves, peeled
2 red chillies, halved
2 tbsp fish sauce
400g/14oz tomatoes, peeled,
   deseeded and chopped
200g/7oz/scant 1 cup caster sugar
5 tbsp rice wine vinegar or white
   wine vinegar

To make the sweet chilli jam, put the ginger, garlic, chillies and fish sauce into a food processor or blender and whizz to a purée. Put the purée in a saucepan with the tomatoes, sugar and vinegar and bring to the boil. Turn the heat down to low and simmer for 15–25 minutes, stirring regularly, until thickened and jam-like in consistency. Pour into sterilized jars, cover with lids and leave to cool, or pour straight into a serving bowl to cool.

To make the fritters, reserve 12 prawns and finely chop the remaining ones. Put the chopped prawns, grated courgettes, chilli, flour, baking powder, spices, spring onions, chopped coriander, salt and eggs into a mixing bowl. Season with pepper and stir until combined into a thick batter consistency.

Heat about 4cm/1½in of oil in a wok or large, deep frying pan until very hot.

Take a dessertspoonful of the prawn mixture in your floured hand, form into a pattie shape and press a whole prawn into the centre. Lower it into the hot oil and continue until you are cooking about 4 fritters at a time. The patties are quite soft but will firm up when cooked. Fry for 2–3 minutes, occasionally spooning the hot oil over the fritters until the prawns are pink and the fritters are golden all over. Drain on kitchen paper and keep warm in a low oven while you continue to cook the remaining fritters; you should have 12 in total.

Serve the fritters with a spoonful of the sweet chilli jam, and with shredded lettuce, spring onions and lime wedges for squeezing over.

HALLOUMI, CHICKPEA & RED ONION SALAD WITH POMEGRANATE MOLASSES DRESSING

The pomegranate molasses dressing gives a delicious sweet, tangy flavour to this chunky Middle Eastern-style salad. The salad is best served when the halloumi is still warm, and you could serve it with pitta or flatbreads.

SERVES 4   PREPARATION TIME: 15 MINUTES   COOKING TIME: 4 MINUTES

1 Cos lettuce, roughly chopped
800g/1lb 12oz canned chickpeas,
  drained and rinsed
1 small red onion, sliced
1 small cucumber, deseeded and diced
300g/10½ oz halloumi cheese, patted
  dry and cut into 8 slices
1 small pomegranate, cut in half and
  seeds removed
2 tbsp chopped mint leaves
2 tbsp chopped coriander leaves

POMEGRANATE MOLASSES DRESSING:
4 tbsp extra virgin olive oil, plus extra
  for brushing
2 tbsp pomegranate molasses or
  pomegranate syrup
1 tsp lemon juice
½ tsp caster sugar
sea salt and freshly ground black pepper

Mix together the ingredients for the dressing in a non-metallic bowl and season with salt and pepper. Leave to one side until ready to use.

Divide the lettuce, chickpeas, red onion and cucumber onto four serving plates. Spoon the dressing over and lightly toss until everything is mixed together.

Heat a large griddle pan over a high heat. Brush the halloumi with a little oil. Reduce the heat a little and griddle the halloumi for about 2 minutes on each side, or until softened and golden in places.

Serve the warm halloumi on the salad and scatter the pomegranate seeds, mint and coriander on the top.

Pomegranate Molasses

A key ingredient in Middle Eastern cooking, pomegranate molasses is a syrupy, tangy reduction of pomegranate juice, sugar and lemon juice. Its sweet-sour flavour and thick, sticky consistency make it a useful addition to marinades, glazes and dressings, and it goes particularly well with poultry, pork, lamb and vegetables.

CHARGRILLED AUBERGINES & SKORTHALIA ON CROSTINI

This is definitely one for garlic lovers! Skorthalia is a rich and creamy Greek sauce-cum-dip made with bread, ground pistachios, lemon juice and more than a hint of garlic. You could scatter some pomegranate seeds over the crostini instead of the parsley, if preferred.

MAKES 8   PREPARATION TIME: 20 MINUTES, PLUS COOLING   COOKING TIME: 5 MINUTES

8 large, thick slices of baguette
200g/7oz chargrilled aubergines in oil,
    drained and sliced if necessary
2 tbsp chopped flat-leaf parsley leaves
green salad, to serve

SKORTHALIA:
150g/5½ oz day-old white bread,
    crusts removed and torn into pieces
50g/1¾oz/scant ⅓ cup unsalted shelled
    pistachios
2 garlic cloves
juice of ½ lemon
3–4 tbsp extra virgin olive oil
sea salt and freshly ground black pepper

Preheat the grill to high. To make the skorthalia, soak the bread in 250ml/9fl oz/1 cup water. Finely chop the pistachios in a food processor and add the soaked bread, garlic and lemon juice. Blend to a smooth, creamy consistency, then gradually pour in the olive oil until thickened to the consistency of mayonnaise. Season with salt and pepper.

Toast the slices of baguette on both sides until golden and leave to cool. Top each with a slice of aubergine and a generous spoonful of skorthalia. Scatter the parsley over before serving with green salad.

LEBANESE CHICKEN WITH SPICED LEMON OIL

This chicken comes with fattoush, a Lebanese salad made from vibrant, crunchy vegetables and pieces of crisp, toasted pitta bread. Here it's dressed in a lightly spiced, aromatic lemon oil.

SERVES 4 (SPICED LEMON OIL MAKES 200ML/7FL OZ/SCANT 1 CUP BOTTLE)
PREPARATION TIME: 30 MINUTES, PLUS 8 HOURS INFUSING   COOKING TIME: 30 MINUTES

3 tbsp za'atar spice mix
8 chicken thighs, each one cut 3 times
sea salt and freshly ground black pepper

FATTOUSH:
1 pitta bread
225g/8oz vine-ripened cherry tomatoes, halved
1 small cucumber, quartered lengthways, deseeded and cut into bite-sized pieces
1 red pepper, deseeded and cut into bite-sized pieces
5 radishes, sliced into rounds
4 tbsp chopped mint leaves

4 tbsp chopped flat-leaf parsley leaves
½ tsp cumin seeds, toasted

SPICED LEMON OIL:
200ml/7fl oz/scant 1 cup extra virgin olive oil
3 strips of pared lemon zest
1 unwaxed lemon, quartered
2 garlic cloves, peeled
2 tsp coriander seeds
1 tsp black peppercorns
1 star anise
2 bay leaves
½ tsp rock salt

To make the lemon oil, put all the ingredients into a pan and warm gently for a few minutes. Remove from the heat, cover and leave for 8 hours in a cool place to allow the flavours to infuse. Remove the garlic and lemon zest, squeeze the juice from the quartered lemon, add it to the oil and discard the quarters. Decant the oil into a sterilized bottle and seal with a lid. It will keep for 2 weeks in a cool, dark place and should be stored in the fridge after opening. It can be used straight after bottling, but its flavour will intensify after a few days.

Preheat the oven to 190°C/375°F/Gas 5. Rub the za'atar over each chicken thigh and season with salt and pepper. Put the thighs in a roasting tin and roast for 20–25 minutes until cooked through.

Meanwhile, make the fattoush. Toast both sides of the pitta bread in a large, heavy-based frying pan until starting to crisp. Remove from the pan, split open and toast the inside of the pitta until crisp. Leave to cool, then break the pitta into large, bite-sized pieces. Put the tomatoes, cucumber, red pepper, radishes and herbs in a serving bowl. Spoon 3 tablespoons of the spiced lemon oil over the top and toss until combined. Sprinkle with the cumin seeds. Before serving, turn the pitta in the salad and serve with the chicken thighs.

Za'atar Spice Mix

Za'atar is a versatile Middle Eastern spice mix, made from ground sumac berries, sesame seeds and herbs in varying proportions. You can buy it ready-made, though it's easy to make your own.

GRIDDLED CHICKEN ON POLENTA WITH SUMMER HERB PESTO

There are many variations on classic pesto, the famous basil sauce from Genoa in Italy. Okay, they may not all be authentic, but many are no less delicious, and especially if they are home-made. In this version, basil is joined by fresh thyme, oregano and chives, and the pine nuts are swapped for pistachios. If you have any left over, store it in a covered container in the fridge, making sure there is a layer of oil covering the pesto to keep it fresh.

**SERVES 4   PREPARATION TIME: 30 MINUTES, PLUS MARINATING
COOKING TIME: 30 MINUTES**

4 skinless, boneless chicken breasts,
  about 175g/6oz each
1.5l/52fl oz/6 cups hot chicken stock
200g/7oz/1⅓ cups polenta
shavings of Parmesan cheese,
  to serve (optional)

MARINADE:
2 tbsp olive oil
1 large garlic clove, sliced
1 tbsp balsamic vinegar
6 long thyme sprigs, leaves removed
sea salt and freshly ground black pepper

SUMMER HERB PESTO:
30g/1oz basil leaves
30g/1oz oregano sprigs, leaves removed
4 long thyme sprigs, leaves removed
30g/1oz/scant ¼ cup unsalted shelled
  pistachios
125ml/4fl oz/½ cup extra virgin olive oil
1 clove garlic, crushed
2 tbsp snipped chives
20g/¾oz Parmesan cheese, finely grated

Put the chicken breasts between two large sheets of cling film and flatten slightly with a meat mallet or the end of a rolling pin; you want the breasts to be of an even thickness. Mix together all the ingredients for the marinade in a large non-metallic dish. Season with salt and pepper and add the chicken. Turn the chicken until it is coated. Leave to marinate, covered, for about 1 hour in the fridge.

To make the pesto, put the basil, oregano, thyme and pistachios in a mini food processor and process until finely chopped. Gradually add the oil and blend until it makes a coarse purée. Spoon the pesto into a bowl and stir in the garlic, chives and Parmesan. Season to taste. Leave to one side until ready to use.

To make the polenta, bring the stock to the boil in a large, heavy-based saucepan and pour in the polenta in a steady stream, stirring. Reduce the heat to a simmer and cook for 25–30 minutes, stirring regularly, until the polenta is smooth and creamy and starting to come away from the sides of the pan.

Meanwhile, griddle the chicken in two batches for about 5 minutes on each side until cooked through and there is no trace of pink in the centre. Leave to rest for 10 minutes, covered with foil, while the polenta finishes cooking. Put the polenta on four serving plates and top with the chicken breasts, spoon a little of the pan juices over and serve with a large spoonful of pesto. Add a small amount of shaved Parmesan, if you like.

GLAZED PORK TENDERLOIN IN CHINESE PLUM SAUCE

Similar in taste and consistency to the classic hoisin sauce, this star anise-infused plum sauce makes a sticky, golden glaze for the pork, but it is equally as good used in a stir-fries or Asian noodle and rice dishes. It will keep for 6 months stored in a cool, dark place and 1 month after opening. Store in the fridge once opened.

SERVES 4 (CHINESE PLUM SAUCE MAKES 2 X 350G/12OZ JARS)
PREPARATION TIME: 30 MINUTES, PLUS MARINATING   COOKING TIME: 1½ HOURS

700g/1lb 9oz pork tenderloin, trimmed
    of any fat and silverskin
sea salt and freshly ground black pepper
steamed Thai jasmine rice and pak choi,
    to serve
sesame seeds, to serve

CHINESE PLUM SAUCE:
1 onion, chopped
5 large garlic cloves, chopped

1 bird's eye chilli, chopped
7.5cm/3in piece of fresh root ginger,
    peeled and grated
400g/14oz dark plums, halved and
    stoned
2 tbsp dark soy sauce
150ml/5fl oz/scant ⅔ cup rice vinegar
2 star anise, ground
225g/8oz/1 cup caster sugar
1 tbsp clear honey

To make the Chinese plum sauce, put the onion, garlic, chilli, ginger, plums, soy sauce, vinegar and star anise in a non-reactive pan. Bring to the boil, then turn the heat down to low and simmer for 25 minutes, stirring occasionally until the plums break down into a pulp.

Pass the plum mixture through a sieve to make a coarse purée and discard the solids that are left. Return the purée to the pan and stir in the sugar and honey. Bring to the boil, turn the heat down and simmer for 20–30 minutes until reduced and thickened to a sauce-like consistency. Spoon into sterilized jars, cover and leave to cool. Alternatively, use a portion of the sauce straight away and pot the rest in a sterilized jar.

Spoon 6 tablespoons of the plum sauce over the pork and leave to marinate, covered, for at least 30 minutes.

Preheat the oven to 180°C/350°F/Gas 4. Put the sauce-covered pork on a piece of foil large enough to make a parcel. Season with salt and pepper, bring together the sides of the foil, scrunch the top to make a loose parcel and put it on a baking tray. Bake for 20 minutes, then transfer the parcel to a plate.

Turn the oven to a high grill setting or preheat the grill to high. Open up the parcel and pour the pork juices into a small pan. Spoon another 3 tablespoons of the sauce over the pork and grill for 5 minutes until golden and glazed on top. Transfer the pork to a warm plate, cover loosely with foil and leave to rest for 5 minutes.

Meanwhile, pour any remaining juices left into the pan containing the first lot of juices and heat through. Serve the pork, sliced on the diagonal, with Jasmine rice and pak choi. Spoon the juices over the top and scatter with sesame seeds.

Garlic & Fennel Mustard

This wholegrain mustard has just the right amount of crunch, along with a hint of garlic and fennel. It's great with the usual suspects, but you can also add it to marinades, sauces and rubs. A stick blender makes easy work of breaking down the mustard seeds, but you could use a mini processor instead.

MAKES 3 X 200G/7OZ JARS   PREPARATION TIME: 20 MINUTES, PLUS 1 MONTH MATURING

125g/4½ oz/scant ⅔ cup yellow mustard seeds
2 tbsp brown mustard seeds
2 tsp fennel seeds
¼ tsp turmeric
2 tsp salt
¼ tsp ground black pepper
300ml/10½ fl oz/scant 1¼ cups cider vinegar
125g/4½ oz/⅔ cup soft light brown sugar
1 large garlic clove, crushed

Put both mustard seeds with the fennel seeds, turmeric, salt and pepper in a tall, narrow beaker or jug. Add half the vinegar and leave for 5 minutes to soften. Then blend the mixture using a stick blender. Blend well, making sure you break up most of the seeds and until the mixture starts to thicken.

Add the remaining vinegar, sugar and garlic and continue to blend until thickened. Check the seasoning and pack into sterilized jars with lids. Cover with a lid and store in a cool, dry place for up to 6 months. The flavour will mellow with time and will be ready to eat in about 1 month.

GARLIC & FENNEL MUSTARD-CRUSTED
LEG OF LAMB WITH ROAST PEARS

The wholegrain mustard not only creates a flavoursome crust when roasted, but also helps to keep the lamb moist and succulent. Serve the lamb in thick slices with the sweet, golden baked pears and all your favourite roast accompaniments.

**SERVES 4   PREPARATION TIME: 15 MINUTES, PLUS MARINATING AND RESTING
COOKING TIME: 1 HOUR 5 MINUTES**

6 tbsp Garlic & Fennel Mustard
  (see page 122)
2 tbsp finely chopped rosemary
2 tbsp olive oil
1.25kg/2lb 12oz half leg of lamb, bone in

2 garlic cloves, cut into matchsticks
2 tbsp balsamic vinegar
4 pears, peeled and halved lengthways
sea salt and freshly ground black pepper

Mix together the mustard, rosemary and half of the olive oil.

Make small, deep cuts into the lamb using a sharp knife or skewer. Insert the matchsticks of garlic into the cuts, pressing them into the lamb, then spread the mustard mixture over in a thick layer. Put the lamb in a roasting tin and leave to marinate, covered, for 1 hour at room temperature. Season generously with salt and pepper.

Preheat the oven to 220°C/425°F/Gas 7. Put a splash of water in the bottom of the roasting tin and roast the lamb for 20 minutes. Reduce the oven temperature to 180°C/350°F/Gas 4 and roast the lamb for a further 10 minutes, then remove from the oven.

Just before you take the lamb out of the oven, mix together the remaining olive oil with the balsamic vinegar. Brush the mixture over the pears and put them around the joint of lamb. Roast for a further 30–35 minutes, occasionally basting the lamb with the juices in the tin, until the meat is cooked but still pink in the centre and the pears are tender.

Cover the tin with foil and leave the lamb to rest for 15 minutes. (You could use the juices in the pan to make a gravy.) Carve the lamb and serve in thick slices with the pears.

TAGLIATA WITH CHIMICHURRI SAUCE

This is a twist on the Italian tagliata, the classic seared steak, rocket and Parmesan salad, but instead of the usual splash of balsamic vinegar to finish the dish, it comes with a new take on chimichurri, which can loosely be described as Argentinian pesto sauce.

SERVES 4   PREPARATION TIME: 20 MINUTES   COOKING TIME: 6 MINUTES

2 steaks, such as rib-eye or sirloin, each about 250g/9oz and 2cm/¾in thick, at room temperature
1 tbsp olive oil
100g/3½oz rocket leaves
2 large vine-ripened tomatoes, quartered, deseeded and diced
50g/1¾oz Parmesan cheese, shaved into thin slices
sea salt and freshly ground black pepper
ciabatta bread, to serve

CHIMICHURRI SAUCE:
1 large handful of basil leaves, chopped
1 tbsp chopped oregano leaves
4 tbsp chopped parsley leaves
2 garlic cloves, crushed
115ml/3¾fl oz/scant ½ cup olive oil
3 tbsp sherry vinegar or red wine vinegar
1 tsp ground coriander
½ tsp dried chilli flakes
½ tsp salt

To make the chimichurri sauce, mix together all the ingredients in a bowl, season with salt and pepper, then leave to one side.

Brush the steaks with the olive oil and season with salt and pepper.

Heat a large griddle pan over a high heat. Sear the steaks for about 2–3 minutes on each side, turning once or twice. Leave to rest, covered with foil, for 5 minutes.

Meanwhile, make the salad. Scatter the rocket and tomatoes over four serving plates. Cut the steak into 1cm/½in slices and put on top of the salad. Spoon as much of the chimichurri sauce over as you like and sprinkle with the Parmesan, before serving with slices of ciabatta.

Chimichurri

Chimichurri is one of the most versatile sauces. In Argentina, it is traditionally served with grilled steak, but it also works well with lamb, chicken, vegetables and seafood. Use as a sauce, marinade, dip or salad dressing, or stir into pasta as you would pesto. Feel free to alter the proportions of the herbs, spices and garlic, as preferred, or even add some chopped tomatoes, roasted red peppers or finely chopped toasted nuts.

Mayonnaise

I learnt to make mayonnaise as a child from my mother and I've been making the same recipe ever since, although I've sometimes added the odd twist over the years. Home-made mayonnaise bears little resemblance to the shop-bought version, and it's really satisfying to make. You need to add the oil very slowly in a steady stream to avoid the mixture curdling. You can whisk the mayonnaise by hand, but a stick blender is very effective. I recommend a light, neutral oil because a strong-flavoured one, such as olive oil, can be bitter and overpowering. Great on its own, mayonnaise makes a superb foundation for other sauces and dips: try adding some Sweet Chilli Jam (see the recipe on page 112), herbs, garlic, anchovies, lemon juice or creamed horseradish – there's a multitude of options.

MAKES 2 X 250G/9OZ JARS   PREPARATION TIME: 10 MINUTES

1 egg
2 tbsp white wine vinegar
2 tbsp Dijon mustard
2 tsp granulated sugar
a pinch each of sea salt and freshly ground black pepper
400ml/14fl oz/generous 1½ cups vegetable oil

Crack the egg into a tall, narrow beaker or jug. Add the vinegar, mustard, sugar, salt and pepper and blend using a stick blender until combined.

Very slowly, pour in the vegetable oil in a steady stream, blending continuously, until the mixture becomes opaque and thickens to a smooth, glossy sauce. Be careful not to add too much oil initially or the mixture may curdle. If it does curdle, you can reclaim it by gradually adding the curdled mixture to a second egg and mustard base and starting again.

Check the seasoning and spoon into two sterilized jars, cover with lids, and store in the fridge for up to 4 weeks.

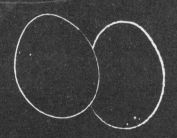

CRAB & PRAWN CAKES WITH SWEET CHILLI **MAYONNAISE**

You could call these posh fishcakes! Buy fresh crabmeat for the best flavour and texture – I've opted for white only as brown can make them too soft. The seafood cakes can be made up to a day in advance and stored in the fridge until ready to cook. Serve with a good spoonful of the sweet chilli mayonnaise. If you don't have enough time to make your own mayo, a good-quality shop-bought version is nearly as good.

SERVES 4   PREPARATION TIME: 30 MINUTES   COOKING TIME: 35 MINUTES

700g/1lb 9oz potatoes, peeled and halved
2 large garlic cloves, cut in half
250g/9oz cooked peeled prawns, roughly chopped
400g/14oz white crabmeat
2 tbsp chopped parsley leaves
2 spring onions, green part only, finely chopped
finely grated zest of 1 small lemon
flour, for dusting
6 tbsp vegetable oil

sea salt and freshly ground black pepper
crisp green salad and lemon wedges, to serve

SWEET CHILLI MAYONNAISE:
125ml/4fl oz/½ cup Mayonnaise (see page 126)
2 tbsp Sweet Chilli Jam (see page 112) or sweet chilli sauce
juice of 1 lime

To make the sweet chilli mayonnaise, mix the mayonnaise with the sweet chilli jam, lime juice and 1–2 tablespoons warm water until combined to a sauce-like consistency. Leave to one side until ready to serve.

Cook the potatoes and garlic in a pan of boiling salted water for 15–20 minutes until tender. Drain the potatoes and garlic in a colander, then return them to the pan to dry in the heat of the pan. Leave to cool slightly, then mash the garlic until smooth and put in a large bowl. Coarsely grate the potatoes into the bowl and season with plenty of salt and pepper.

Add the prawns, crabmeat, parsley, spring onions and lemon zest to the bowl and stir until combined.

Coat a serving plate with a good layer of flour and dust your hands. Divide the potato mixture into 8 and form each portion into a round cake about 2cm/¾in thick. Lightly dust each cake in flour and put on a plate. You can either chill the seafood cakes at this stage or cook them straight away.

Heat half the vegetable oil in a large, non-stick frying pan over a medium heat. Fry the seafood cakes in two batches for about 4 minutes on each side until golden and crisp, adding more oil when necessary. Drain on kitchen paper and keep the seafood cakes warm in a low oven while you cook the second batch. Serve with the sweet chilli mayonnaise, a crisp green salad and lemon wedges.

HARISSA & TOMATO COUSCOUS WITH LEMONY ROASTED VEGETABLES

Fans of harissa, the fiery North African paste, will love this dish as it not only adds heaps of flavour to the couscous and accompanying mayonnaise, but is also a wonderful warm colour.

SERVES 4   PREPARATION TIME: 20 MINUTES   COOKING TIME: 40 MINUTES

175g/6oz cherry tomatoes on the vine
4 large garlic cloves
1 aubergine, thinly sliced lengthways
2 courgettes, thinly sliced lengthways
2 red onions, peeled and cut into wedges
2 romano red peppers, deseeded and
    quartered lengthways
4 tbsp Spiced Lemon Oil (see page 116)
175g/6oz jarred chargrilled artichokes
250g/9oz/heaped 1⅓ cups couscous

400ml/14fl oz/generous 1½ cups
    just-boiled, good-quality chicken stock
2 tsp harissa paste
100g/3½ oz/⅔ cup blanched almonds
1 handful of basil leaves (optional)
sea salt and freshly ground black pepper

HARISSA MAYO:
2 tsp harissa paste
4 tbsp good-quality mayonnaise

Preheat the oven to 200°C/400°F/Gas 6. Divide the tomatoes, garlic, aubergine, courgettes, onions and peppers between two large roasting tins. Generously brush with lemon oil and roast for 20 minutes until the tomatoes and garlic are soft. Remove, turn the vegetables, add the artichokes, brush with more lemon oil, if necessary, then return to the oven for 20 minutes until the vegetables are tender and blackened in places.

While the vegetables are roasting, put the couscous in a heatproof bowl, pour the chicken stock over, stir, then cover. Set aside for 5 minutes, or until the couscous has absorbed the stock, then fluff up with a fork.

Remove the cherry tomatoes from the vines and peel the roasted garlic. Put the tomatoes and garlic in a mini food processor with 1 tablespoon of the lemon oil and the harissa. Process to make a smooth sauce, season with salt and pepper, then stir it into the cooked couscous. Cover with a plate and leave to one side. Toast the almonds in a dry frying pan over a medium heat for 5 minutes, turning once, until starting to turn golden. Mix together the ingredients for the harissa mayo with 1 teaspoon warm water. Scatter the almonds over the couscous and serve topped with the vegetables, the harissa mayo and a few basil leaves, if you like.

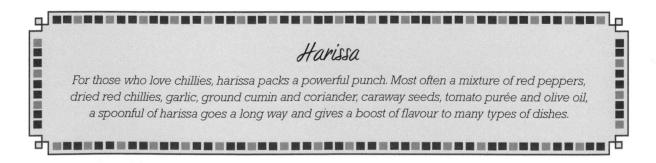

Harissa

For those who love chillies, harissa packs a powerful punch. Most often a mixture of red peppers, dried red chillies, garlic, ground cumin and coriander, caraway seeds, tomato purée and olive oil, a spoonful of harissa goes a long way and gives a boost of flavour to many types of dishes.

5. Vegetables

Preserved Mushrooms in Oil

These mushrooms take on a hint of the lemon and herbs but retain their woody, earthy flavours.
Serve them as part of an antipasti, as a topping for bruschetta or as a simple pasta sauce.

MAKES 1L/35FL OZ/4 CUP JAR   PREPARATION TIME: 10 MINUTES, PLUS 3 DAYS MATURING
COOKING TIME: 13 MINUTES

115ml/3¾fl oz/scant ½ cup cider vinegar
3 garlic cloves, halved
6 long thyme sprigs
4 long rosemary sprigs
2 tsp rock salt
1 tsp black peppercorns
750g/1lb 10oz mixed mushrooms of varying size and type, such as baby button, chestnut, enoki,
shiitake, oyster, girolles or chanterelles, wiped of any dirt and stalks trimmed if necessary
pared zest of ½ unwaxed lemon
2 bay leaves
good-quality olive oil, about 375ml/13fl oz/1½ cups, to cover

Combine the vinegar, 500ml/17fl oz/2 cups water, the garlic, half the thyme and rosemary, the salt
and peppercorns in a large, non-reactive pan. Bring to the boil, then turn the heat down and stir until
the salt dissolves. Add the mushrooms, then simmer for 10 minutes or until softened and cooked.
Strain well through a sieve and remove the garlic, thyme and rosemary. Discard the vinegar mixture.
Put the mushrooms, peppercorns, zest, bay leaves and reserved thyme and rosemary in a sterilized jar.
Pour in the oil to cover, then use a wooden skewer to get rid of air pockets and seal with a lid.
Store in a cool, dark place for up to 2 weeks and store in the fridge after opening.
They can be eaten after 2 days and are best eaten within 2 weeks.

POLENTA BRUSCHETTA WITH **PRESERVED MUSHROOMS** & SMOKED DUCK

Slices of grilled crisp polenta make a refreshing alternative to bruschetta made with crusty bread and provide the perfect base to this mushroom and smoked duck topping. Feel free to swap the duck for an alternative cooked or cured meat or poultry: ham, salami, chorizo or slices of roast chicken, beef or lamb would all work.

SERVES 4   PREPARATION TIME: 10 MINUTES, PLUS SETTING   COOKING TIME: 25 MINUTES

¼ recipe quantity Preserved Mushrooms in Oil (see page 132), drained
2 smoked skinless duck breasts, cut into strips
2 tbsp chopped parsley leaves

POLENTA BRUSCHETTA:
175g/6oz/scant 1¼ cups instant polenta
40g/1½ oz butter
50g/1¾oz/½ cup finely grated Parmesan cheese
olive oil, for greasing and brushing
sea salt and freshly ground black pepper

To make the polenta bruschetta, put 850ml/29fl oz/scant 3½ cups water in a saucepan, gradually stir in the polenta and bring to the boil. Turn the heat down to low and simmer for 10 minutes, stirring until thickened to a smooth paste and starting to come away from the sides of the pan. Remove from the heat and stir in the butter and Parmesan. Season to taste with salt and pepper.

Lightly oil a baking tray and spread the polenta into an even layer, about 2cm/¾in thick. Smooth the top and leave to cool and set.

Preheat the grill to high. Cut the polenta into 4 squares, then cut each square into a triangle. Brush the polenta with a little olive oil, put on a grill rack and grill for 12 minutes, turning once, until crisp and golden on the outside. Top the polenta with a large spoonful of the preserved mushrooms, a few slices of duck and a sprinkling of parsley. Season with salt and pepper and serve warm.

Types of Polenta

Golden yellow polenta makes a great alternative to bread, potatoes, rice or pasta. The ground corn comes in various forms: traditional coarsely ground polenta takes a while to cook but I think it has the best flavour, then there's the super-quick finely ground instant polenta, as well as the ready-made polenta sold in slabs ready to be sliced and fried, grilled or chargrilled.

ROASTED RED PEPPER GAZPACHO WITH SERRANO CRISPS

Choose the most flavoursome, fragrant, vine-ripened tomatoes that you can find and you'll be rewarded with the best-tasting gazpacho.

SERVES 4   PREPARATION TIME: 25 MINUTES, PLUS CHILLING   COOKING TIME: 25 MINUTES

2 romano red peppers
1kg/2lb 4oz large vine-ripened tomatoes
2 slices of day-old bread, crusts removed
1 cucumber, peeled, deseeded and chopped
1 green chilli, deseeded and chopped
1 garlic clove
3 tbsp extra virgin olive oil
juice of 1 lime and 1 lemon
1 tsp caster sugar

a few drops of Tabasco sauce
4–6 slices of Serrano ham
1 handful of basil leaves, for sprinkling
sea salt and freshly ground black pepper

CROÛTONS:
2 slices of day-old bread, crusts removed
1 garlic clove, halved lengthways
2 tbsp olive oil

Preheat the grill to high. Grill the peppers for 15 minutes, turning them occasionally, until softened and blackened in places. Put the peppers in a plastic bag and leave for 5 minutes (this will make the skins easier to remove). Remove the skin and seeds and leave to one side.

Meanwhile, using a small, sharp knife, cut a shallow cross in the bottom of each tomato, then put them in a heatproof bowl and cover with just-boiled water. Leave to stand for 2 minutes, then drain. Peel off and discard the tomato skins, then deseed and cut the flesh into large chunks.

Soak the bread in 150ml/5fl oz/scant ⅔ cup water in a shallow dish for 5 minutes. Remove the bread from the dish (it will have absorbed most of the water) and tear into chunks.

Put half the soaked bread, roasted peppers, tomatoes, cucumber, chilli, garlic, extra virgin olive oil, lime and lemon juice in a blender with 200ml/7fl oz/scant 1 cup cold water and blend until combined but chunky. Repeat with the remaining ingredients and another 200ml/7fl oz/scant 1 cup cold water. Combine the two batches in a large jug, stir in the sugar and a few drops of Tabasco and season. Chill, covered, for 2–3 hours.

To make the croûtons, rub the bread slices with the cut side of the garlic cloves. Cut the bread into cubes and put them in a small plastic bag with the oil. Seal the bag and shake gently to coat the bread in the olive oil. Heat a large, non-stick frying pan and fry the croûtons over a medium heat for 6–8 minutes until crisp and golden all over. Leave to drain on kitchen paper.

Wipe the frying pan clean and add the ham in a single layer. Cook for 3 minutes, or until crisp, turning once. Leave to cool slightly, then break into large bite-sized pieces. Ladle the soup into bowls and scatter the croûtons, Serrano crisps and basil leaves over before serving.

PEA, BACON & SCAMORZA FRITTATAS

The natural sweetness of the peas and courgette work well with the salty smokiness of the bacon and scamorza in these individual frittatas. Scamorza is a type of mozzarella (see page 74) and the smoked version (affumicata) is used here. It can be recognized by its golden-brown rind and its unique pear shape, which is due to the way the cheese is hung.

MAKES 4–6   PREPARATION TIME: 15 MINUTES   COOKING TIME: 30 MINUTES

melted butter, for greasing
450g/1lb potatoes, such as Maris Piper, peeled and cut into 2cm/¾in chunks
2 tsp olive oil
3 back bacon rashers, rind removed and roughly chopped
2 spring onions, green part only, finely chopped

1 small courgette, coarsely grated
100g/3½ oz/⅔ cup frozen petit pois
100g/3½ oz scamorza affumicata (smoked) cheese, diced
4 tbsp finely grated Parmesan cheese
8 eggs, lightly beaten
sea salt and freshly ground black pepper
crusty bread and tomato salad, to serve

Preheat the oven to 190°C/375°F/Gas 5. Line four holes of a deep muffin tin with 15cm/6in squares of baking paper, folding the paper to fit the hole; the paper case should rise above the top of the tin but may need trimming slightly. (Or you could use the large, ready-made paper cases labelled as "designer" cases in larger supermarkets.) Brush the paper cases with a little melted butter. (Alternatively, if not using the paper cases, lightly butter six holes of a deep muffin tin.)

Cook the potatoes in a pan of boiling salted water for 8–10 minutes until tender. Drain and leave to cool in a large bowl.

Meanwhile, heat the olive oil in a large, non-stick frying pan over a medium heat. Cook the bacon for 5 minutes until lightly browned and starting to crisp. Remove using a slotted spoon and drain on kitchen paper, then add the spring onions and courgette to the pan and cook for another minute until softened.

Cook the peas in a pan of boiling water until tender, then drain and refresh under cold running water. Add the peas to the bowl containing the potatoes with the bacon, spring onions, courgette, scamorza and Parmesan. Spoon the mixture into the prepared muffin tin.

Season the beaten eggs with salt and pepper and pour in the prepared tin. Stir each frittata gently with a fork until everything is combined. Bake for 20 minutes, or until risen and set. Leave the frittatas in the muffin tin for 5 minutes, then serve warm or at room temperature with crusty bread and tomato salad.

Piccalilli

This is one of our bestselling condiments at Bay Tree and it's our take on the classic version, using some of the core ingredients but adding an extra twist. This is a must with cold meats and cheese and it goes particularly well with a really good pork pie.

**MAKES 3 X 250G/9OZ JARS   PREPARATION TIME: 15 MINUTES, PLUS COOLING
COOKING TIME: 15 MINUTES**

85ml/2¾fl oz/⅓ cup cider vinegar
100g/3½oz/scant ½ cup granulated sugar
100g/3½oz American-style mustard
½ tsp ginger purée
½ tsp turmeric
1 carrot, about 80g/2¾oz total weight, diced
80g/2¾oz green beans, cut into 2cm/¾in pieces
1 small green pepper, deseeded and diced
1 small red pepper, deseeded and diced
1½ tbsp cornflour
½ cauliflower, about 80g/2¾oz total weight, cut into small florets

Mix together the vinegar, sugar, mustard, ginger and turmeric in a large non-reactive pan and bring to the boil. Add the carrot and beans and return to the boil, then stir in the green and red peppers.

Mix the cornflour into 3 tablespoons water and stir this into the pan with the cauliflower. Return to the boil, then turn the heat down and simmer for 5 minutes until the mixture has thickened but the vegetables remain crunchy.

Remove the pan from the heat and spoon the mixture into sterilized jars while still hot. Cover with lids and leave to cool.

The piccalilli can be eaten once cold but is best left for a few weeks to allow the flavours to mature and the vegetables to soften. Keep in a cool, dark place for up to 4 months, then store in the fridge for up to 1 month once opened.

SOUSED MACKEREL WITH **PICCALILLI** REMOULADE

Reminiscent of days gone by, sousing is simply a form of pickling fish to preserve it. Herring and sardines will work here, too, but whichever type of fish you choose it must be really fresh.

**SERVES 4   PREPARATION TIME: 20 MINUTES, PLUS OVERNIGHT SOUSING
COOKING TIME: 5 MINUTES**

4 juniper berries, bruised with the blade
   of a knife
½ tsp black peppercorns
2 bay leaves
1 tsp sea salt
1 tsp caraway seeds, toasted
4 shallots, sliced into rounds
finely grated zest and juice of 1 lemon
200ml/7fl oz/scant 1 cup cider vinegar
100g/3½ oz/½ cup soft light brown sugar
4 mackerel fillets
watercress and slices of rye bread, to serve

REMOULADE:
200g/7oz celeriac, peeled and cut into
   thin matchsticks using a mandolin or
   coarsely grated
juice of 1 lemon
1 uncooked beetroot, peeled and coarsely
   grated
5 tablespoons mayonnaise
3 tablespoons Piccalilli (see page 138)
2 tbsp crème fraîche
2 tbsp chopped parsley leaves
sea salt and freshly ground black pepper

Put all the listed ingredients from the juniper berries to the brown sugar in a saucepan and bring to the boil.

Put the mackerel in a single layer in a non-metallic shallow dish; they should fit quite snugly. Pour the hot vinegar mixture over the fish, cover with cling film and leave to cool. The fish will cook slightly in the heat of the vinegar. Once cool, leave the fish overnight in the fridge to souse (marinate).

Just before serving, make the remoulade. Toss the prepared celeriac in lemon juice to prevent it discolouring. Combine the celeriac with the beetroot in a serving bowl. Mix together the mayonnaise, piccalilli and crème fraîche with 1 tablespoon warm water. Season to taste with salt and pepper and spoon the dressing over the celeriac and beetroot. Stir until combined and scatter the parsley over the top.

Remove the mackerel from the sousing liquid and serve with a good spoonful of the remoulade, with watercress and slices of rye bread.

Sousing

Sousing involves soaking fish fillets in a hot brine of vinegar, sugar, salt and flavourings, firming and curing the flesh, and giving the fish a zingy, sweet-sour taste. This will keep in the fridge for 3–4 days.

CARPACCIO OF FENNEL WITH PRAWNS & MARINATED OLIVES

This light salad reminds me of summer with its beautiful fresh, invigorating flavours. The quantity of marinated olives is greater than you need for the recipe but they can be kept for up to 1 week if stored, covered, in the fridge.

**SERVES 4 PREPARATION TIME: 20 MINUTES, PLUS MARINATING
COOKING TIME: 3 MINUTES**

2 tsp paprika
500g/1lb 2oz frozen raw, peeled king
  prawns, defrosted
1 tbsp olive oil
2 large fennel bulbs, trimmed
2 tbsp chopped coriander leaves
sea salt and freshly ground black pepper

MARINATED OLIVES:
finely grated zest and juice of 1 orange
4 tbsp extra virgin olive oil
1 tbsp white wine vinegar
1 red chilli, deseeded and diced
1 large garlic clove, thinly sliced
2 tsp fennel seeds, toasted
200g/7oz/1½ cups Niçoise olives

Strain the orange juice to remove any bits and mix with the zest, extra virgin olive oil, vinegar, chilli, garlic and fennel seeds. Reserve 3 tablespoons of the marinade to use as a dressing and pour the remaining mixture over the olives. Stir until combined and leave to marinate for at least 1 hour.

Sprinkle the paprika over the prawns and season with salt and pepper. Heat the olive oil in a large frying pan over a medium heat and cook the prawns for about 3 minutes, or until pink and cooked through. Leave to cool slightly.

Prepare the salad just before serving. Using a mandolin or a sharp knife, cut the fennel bulbs into thin slices and put on a serving plate. Top with the prawns and spoon the reserved dressing over.

Using a slotted spoon, scoop out as many olives as you like. Scatter the olives and coriander over the top of the salad and serve straight away.

Olives

Olives are too bitter to eat straight from the tree and must be cured to make them edible. Many olives start off green and become black when ripe, although this isn't strictly true of all varieties, of which there are hundreds in various sizes and shades of colour, ranging from the Greek purple Kalamata to the French black Niçoise and Spanish green Manzanilla.

WHITE ONION & SAGE FARINATA WITH SPINACH TZATZIKI

Farinata is a thin, savoury chickpea flour cake with the consistency of a pancake. With its origins in Liguria, north-western Italy, it's so popular that bakeries often have a sign in the window to tell customers when the farinata is ready. Usually sold plain, this version is flavoured with slices of sweet white onion, olives, chilli and sage.

SERVES 4   PREPARATION TIME: 15 MINUTES, PLUS STANDING   COOKING TIME: 25 MINUTES

150g/5½ oz/1⅓ cups chickpea flour
½ tsp salt
1 large egg, lightly beaten
5 tbsp olive oil
1 white onion, thinly sliced into rounds
1 red chilli, deseeded and sliced
55g/2oz/⅓ cup pitted black olives, halved
1 heaped tbsp chopped sage

SPINACH TZATZIKI:
200g/7oz spinach leaves, tough stalks
  removed
185ml/6fl oz/¾ cup natural yogurt
1 small clove garlic, crushed
1 tbsp lemon juice
sea salt and freshly ground black pepper

Mix together the chickpea flour and salt in a mixing bowl. Make a well in the centre and stir in the egg, 2 tablespoons of the olive oil and 400ml/14fl oz/generous 1½ cups lukewarm water. Using a wooden spoon, gradually draw the flour into the wet ingredients and stir to make a thick, smooth batter. Cover and leave to stand for 1 hour.

Meanwhile, make the spinach tzatziki. Steam the spinach for 2 minutes or until wilted. Drain well, then press the spinach with the back of a wooden spoon to squeeze out any excess water.

Mix together the yogurt, garlic, 4 tablespoons water and lemon juice and season to taste with salt and pepper. Unravel the spinach and stir it into the yogurt mixture. Cover and chill until needed.

Preheat the oven to 220°C/425°F/Gas 7. Pour the remaining olive oil into a 33 x 23cm/13 x 9in non-stick baking tray and heat in the oven for 4 minutes until very hot. Carefully remove the tray from the oven.

Stir the batter and pour it into the baking tray and scatter the onion, chilli, olives and sage over the top. Bake for 15–20 minutes until set and golden. Cut into squares and serve warm with the spinach tzatziki.

Cherry Tomato & Thyme Sweet Pickle

Pickling in sweetened vinegar concentrates the flavour of the cherry tomatoes, making them intensely "tomatoey" and succulent. Great with cheeses, pâtés, cold meats and pies, the pickle also makes a stunning gift.

**MAKES 500G/1LB 2OZ JAR   PREPARATION TIME: 10 MINUTES, PLUS INFUSING
COOKING TIME: 10 MINUTES**

3 tbsp coriander seeds, slightly crushed
400ml/14fl oz/generous 1½ cups white wine vinegar
400g/14oz/heaped 1¾ cups granulated sugar
600g/1lb 5oz mixed vine-ripened yellow and red cherry tomatoes
6 long thyme sprigs

Put the coriander seeds in a small muslin bag in a non-reactive pan with the vinegar and sugar. Bring to the boil, then turn the heat down and simmer, stirring, until the sugar dissolves. Remove the pan from the heat and leave for 30 minutes to allow the coriander seeds to infuse the sweetened vinegar.

Meanwhile, prick the tomatoes all over using a wooden cocktail stick and pack into the sterilized jar with the thyme. Remove the muslin bag from the vinegar and pour it over the tomatoes. Cover with a lid – you may need to weight the tomatoes down to prevent them floating above the sweet vinegar, but make sure whatever you use is cleaned and sterilized.

You can eat the pickle straight away but it is best left for at least 1 week. Ideally, keep in a cool, dark place for about 1 month, then store in the fridge once opened. Once open, eat within 2 weeks.

GOAT'S CHEESE & CHIVE GALETTES WITH
CHERRY TOMATO & THYME PICKLE

The milky acidity of the goat's cheese works brilliantly with the sweet-sour flavour of the pickled tomatoes. Served with a crisp green salad, these puff pastry galettes make a delicious summery lunch or a delightful addition to a picnic.

SERVES 4   PREPARATION TIME: 15 MINUTES   COOKING TIME: 20 MINUTES

extra virgin olive oil, for greasing and
   drizzling
320g/11¼ oz ready-rolled puff pastry
flour, for dusting
300g/10½ oz chèvre blanc cheese,
   rind removed
2 garlic cloves, crushed
2 tbsp snipped chives

1 small egg, beaten
4 vine-ripened tomatoes, sliced into rounds
¼ recipe quantity Cherry Tomato & Thyme
   Sweet Pickle, drained (see page 142)
100g/3½ oz pea shoots
sea salt and freshly ground black pepper
crisp green salad, to serve

Preheat the oven to 200°C/400°F/Gas 6 and oil a large baking tray. Put the pastry on a lightly floured surface and cut into 4 rectangles, about 17 x 12cm/6½ x 4½in. Score a line about 1cm/½in in from the edge.

Crumble the goat's cheese into a bowl and stir in the garlic and chives. Season to taste. Sprinkle the cheese mixture over each pastry base, leaving a border around the edge. Brush the edge of the pastry with a little egg and put on a baking tray. Top with the sliced tomatoes, drizzle with a little extra virgin olive oil and bake for 15–20 minutes, or until the pastry is cooked and golden. Meanwhile, cut the pickled cherry tomatoes in half. Remove the galettes from the oven and leave to cool slightly. Top each galette with a pile of pea shoots and the pickled tomatoes just before serving hot or cold with a green salad.

Oven-Roasted Tomatoes

These are just so good, and the perfect way to use up a glut of tomatoes. The slow-roasting concentrates the flavour of the tomatoes and gives them a slightly chewy texture. You could store them in an airtight container or pack in a sterilized jar and cover with olive oil. Use the tomatoes within 1 month – if they last that long!

**MAKES 500G/1LB 2OZ   PREPARATION TIME: 15 MINUTES, PLUS DRAINING
COOKING TIME: 2½ HOURS**

1kg/2lb 4oz vine-ripened tomatoes, cut in half lengthways
3 garlic cloves, thinly sliced
4 tbsp olive oil
6 long oregano sprigs, leaves removed
sea salt and freshly ground black pepper
extra virgin olive oil, to cover (optional)

Using a teaspoon, scoop out the seeds from the tomatoes, leaving a hollow tomato shell. Sprinkle the insides of each tomato lightly with salt and put, cut-side down, on a wire rack over a baking tray. Leave for 1 hour to drain, then rinse and pat dry with kitchen paper.

Preheat the oven to 110°C/225°F/Gas ½. Put the tomatoes, cut-side up, on two baking trays. Sprinkle the tomatoes with the garlic, olive oil and oregano. Season with a little salt and pepper and roast the tomatoes for 2–2½ hours, or until they look wrinkly and almost dry. Use straight away or leave to cool, then transfer to an airtight container or pack in a sterilized jar and cover with extra virgin olive oil. Store in the fridge.

CHICKEN BROCHETTES WITH ARTICHOKE & **OVEN-ROASTED TOMATO** CONFIT

The saffron-infused stock is simmered over a low heat until reduced to an unctuous sauce for the artichokes, olives and Oven-Roasted Tomatoes. You could use fresh baby artichoke hearts instead of the jarred variety, if preferred. Remove the artichoke leaves and scoop out the hearts. Discard the leaves and hairy choke, then cook the hearts in boiling salted water until tender.

**SERVES 4   PREPARATION TIME: 20 MINUTES, PLUS MARINATING
COOKING TIME: 30 MINUTES**

CHICKEN BROCHETTES:
150ml/5fl oz/scant ⅔ cup natural yogurt
1 tsp turmeric
2 garlic cloves, crushed
½ red chilli, diced
juice of ½ lemon
550g/1lb 4oz skinless, boneless chicken
   breasts, cut into 16 bite-sized pieces
1 large red onion, cut into wedges
6 large bay leaves, halved lengthways
olive oil, for brushing
sea salt and freshly ground black pepper
1 tbsp roughly chopped parsley leaves
slices of ciabatta, to serve

ARTICHOKE AND OVEN-ROASTED
   TOMATO CONFIT:
a large pinch of saffron threads
4 tbsp extra virgin olive oil
4 large garlic cloves, sliced
250g/9oz chargrilled artichoke hearts in
   oil, drained and halved if large
½ recipe quantity Oven-Roasted Tomatoes
   (see pages 144)
100g/3½ oz/scant 1 cup pitted Kalamata
   olives
50g/1¾oz Preserved Lemons (see page
   166), drained and finely chopped

Mix together the yogurt, turmeric, garlic, chilli and lemon juice in a non-metallic dish. Season with salt and pepper and add the chicken. Turn the chicken in the yogurt marinade and leave to marinate, covered, for 1 hour in the fridge.

Thread 4 pieces of chicken on a long metal skewer, alternating with a few slices of onion and 3 bay leaf halves, starting and ending with the onion. Repeat to make 4 skewers in total. Cover and chill until required.

To make the confit, soak the saffron threads in 300ml/10½fl oz/scant 1¼ cups hot water. Heat the oil in a wide, deep frying pan and fry the garlic for 1 minute, then add the saffron stock and artichokes. Bring to the boil, then turn the heat down to low and simmer for 15–20 minutes until it has reduced by two-thirds.

Stir in the oven-roasted tomatoes, olives and preserved lemons and heat through for another 5 minutes until the stock has thickened to a sauce-like consistency. Add an extra splash of oil and/or water if the confit appears dry. Season with salt and pepper to taste.

Meanwhile, preheat the grill to high and line the grill pan with foil. Brush the chicken brochettes with olive oil and grill for 8–10 minutes, turning occasionally, until golden in places and cooked through. Serve the brochettes with the confit. Sprinkle with parsley and serve with slices of ciabatta.

STUFFED TAPENADE CHICKEN

We started making olive paste, or tapenade, after being asked by a customer. Our first recipe went down so well that we then started to make additional flavours. This one is delicious as part of an antipasti, mixed into pasta, spooned onto bruschetta or used as a stuffing, as in this recipe.

SERVES 4 (TAPENADE MAKES 3 X 200G/7OZ JARS)   PREPARATION TIME: 20 MINUTES   COOKING TIME: 35 MINUTES

olive oil, for greasing and brushing
4 skinless, boneless chicken breasts, about 175g/6oz each
115g/4oz mozzarella cheese, drained, patted dry and sliced
4 slices of San Danielle ham
sea salt and freshly ground black pepper
roasted new potatoes or baked potato wedges and green vegetables such as tenderstem broccoli, to serve

MUSHROOM AND OLIVE TAPENADE:
235g/8½ oz/2 cups black olives, pitted and cut into wedges
150g/5½ oz/¾ cup green olives, pitted and chopped
2 tbsp olive oil
1 small onion, diced
175g/6oz mushrooms, finely chopped
75g/2½ oz sun-dried tomato paste
3 large garlic cloves, crushed

To make the tapenade, reserve 15g/½oz of the black olives. Using a stick blender, purée the remaining black olives with the green olives. Leave to one side.

Heat the olive oil in a pan and cook the onion over a low heat for 10 minutes until very soft. Add the mushrooms, tomato paste, garlic, then season with black pepper and simmer until any liquid boils away and the mixture thickens to a paste consistency.

Stir in the olive purée and the reserved black olives and boil for 1 minute until heated through. Pack into sterilized jars, cover with lids and leave to cool. Store in the fridge once made and use within 1 month.

Preheat the oven to 190°C/375°F/Gas 5 and lightly oil a baking dish. Make a cut along one side of each chicken breast and open out to make a long, deep pocket. Spread 1 tablespoon of the tapenade in each pocket and top it with the mozzarella. Wrap a slice of ham around each chicken breast to seal in the filling, brush with olive oil and season with salt and pepper.

Put the stuffed chicken breasts in the prepared baking dish and roast for 18–20 minutes until cooked through and there is no trace of pink in the centre. Serve with roasted new potatoes and green vegetables.

PERSIAN LAMB CUTLETS WITH AUBERGINE CAVIAR & BEETROOT CRISPS

The aubergines are roasted until meltingly tender and then mashed with garlic and herbs until smooth and creamy. The "caviar" is delicious with the lamb, coated in a Persian spice mix known as advieh. You might be lucky enough to find heritage beetroot with its vibrant candy colours of yellow, ruby red and orange to make the crisps, in which case all the better.

SERVES 4   PREPARATION TIME: 25 MINUTES   COOKING TIME: 1 HOUR 20 MINUTES

3 uncooked beetroots, peeled and thinly
   sliced, about 3mm/⅛ in thick
2 tbsp olive oil, plus extra for brushing
8–12 lamb cutlets, depending on size
sea salt and freshly ground black pepper

PERSIAN SPICE MIX:
2 tsp cardamom seeds, about 14 pods
2 tsp each of coriander seeds, cumin
   seeds, turmeric, ground ginger and
   dried mint

1 tsp ground nutmeg
1 tsp salt

AUBERGINE CAVIAR:
2 large aubergines
olive oil, for brushing
6 large garlic cloves
juice of 1 lemon
2 tbsp extra virgin olive oil
1 handful of mint, leaves chopped
1 handful of parsley, leaves chopped

Preheat the oven to 190°C/375°F/Gas 5. Pierce the aubergines all over with a skewer, then put them in a roasting dish. Brush the aubergines with olive oil and scatter the garlic around. Roast for 30 minutes, or until the garlic is soft. Remove the garlic from the dish, turn the aubergines and return them to the oven for another 30 minutes. Mash the garlic to a purée using the back of a fork.

Meanwhile, lightly brush both sides of the beetroots with a little olive oil and season with salt and pepper. Put on a baking sheet and roast at the same time as the aubergine for 20–25 minutes, turning once, until just crisp – take care as they can easily burn and they will crisp up further when cool. Drain on kitchen paper and leave to one side.

Mix together all the ingredients for the spice mix, then rub enough of the mixture over both sides of each lamb cutlet. Save any remaining spice mix in an airtight container for future use. Remove the aubergine from the oven and leave until cool enough to handle.

Heat the olive oil in a large frying pan over a high heat and sear the lamb in two or three batches for 2 minutes on each side until golden. Transfer the lamb to a large roasting dish and transfer to the oven and cook for about 5 minutes; the lamb should still be pink in the centre.

Meanwhile, peel the skin off the aubergines, chop into pieces, add to the bowl with the roasted garlic and mash to a purée. Stir in the lemon juice and extra virgin olive oil and season to taste with salt and pepper. Fold in the herbs. Serve the caviar topped with the lamb cutlets and scatter the beetroot crisps around.

BEEF, PORCINI & CHESTNUT BOURGUIGNON

This is a rich, comforting stew packed with flavour from the dried porcini mushrooms, red wine, garlic, stock and beef. Creamy mashed potatoes are a must for soaking up the meaty gravy.

SERVES 4   PREPARATION TIME: 20 MINUTES, PLUS SOAKING   COOKING TIME: 2½ HOURS

15g/½ oz dried porcini mushrooms
2 tbsp olive oil
750g/1lb 10oz braising steak, trimmed of fat and cut into large bite-sized pieces
200g/7oz shallots, peeled and halved, if large
3 garlic cloves, chopped
2 tbsp plain flour
350ml/12fl oz/scant 1½ cups red wine
100ml/3½ fl oz/generous ⅓ cup beef stock

250g/9oz chestnut mushrooms, halved, if large
6 thyme sprigs
1 bay leaf
1cm/½ in strip of pared unwaxed orange zest
200g/7oz tinned cooked chestnuts, halved
1 tbsp Worcestershire sauce
sea salt and freshly ground black pepper

Soak the porcini mushrooms in 6 tablespoons hot water for 20 minutes until softened. Strain the porcini mushrooms, reserving the soaking liquor.

Heat half the olive oil in a large flameproof casserole over a medium heat. Season the beef and sear in two or three batches until browned, adding more oil when necessary. Remove from the pan and leave to one side. Add the shallots and sauté, covered, for 10 minutes until softened, stirring occasionally. Add the garlic and cook for another minute.

Return the seared beef to the casserole, stir in the flour, then cook for a couple of minutes, stirring. Pour in the wine and deglaze the casserole by scraping up any bits stuck to the bottom. Let the wine bubble gently for 5 minutes until reduced. Add the soaked porcini and soaking liquor, the stock, mushrooms, thyme, bay leaf and orange zest and bring to the boil, then turn the heat down and simmer, part-covered, for 1¼ hours, stirring occasionally.

Add the chestnuts and Worcestershire sauce, cover and simmer for another 30–40 minutes until the beef is extremely tender and the sauce has reduced and thickened. Add more stock during this time if the stew appears dry or remove the lid if there is too much sauce. Season to taste with salt and pepper and serve.

Dried Mushrooms

Dried mushrooms, such as porcini, shiitake and morels, keep for ages and, after briefly rehydrating in hot water, they add an intense flavour to all sorts of dishes.

SEAFOOD & RED PEPPER TAGINE

Roasting sweetens and caramelizes the natural sugars in the red peppers as well as concentrating their flavour, lending a slight smokiness. Long, pointed romano red peppers have a more intense flavour but you can use bell peppers instead, if preferred.

**SERVES 4   PREPARATION TIME: 20 MINUTES, PLUS MARINATING
COOKING TIME: 55 MINUTES**

2 romano red peppers
2 tsp ground cumin
1 tbsp ground coriander
3 garlic cloves, crushed
juice of 1 lime
600g/1lb 5oz thick, skinless, boneless white fish, such as pollock, cod, haddock or monkfish, cut into large bite-sized pieces
250g/9oz raw, peeled king prawns
400g/14oz new potatoes, halved or quartered if large
2 tbsp olive oil

1 onion, sliced
5cm/2in piece of fresh root ginger, peeled and grated
4 long thyme sprigs
400g/14oz/scant 1⅔ cups tinned chopped tomatoes
250ml/9fl oz/1 cup good-quality fish stock
1 tsp harissa paste, or to taste
75g/2½ oz/generous ½ cup Niçoise olives
sea salt and freshly ground black pepper
couscous, coriander leaves and lime wedges, to serve

Preheat the oven to 200°C/400°F/Gas 6. Put the peppers on a baking sheet lined with baking paper and roast for 35–40 minutes until softened. Put the peppers in a plastic bag and leave for 5 minutes (this will make the skins easier to remove). Remove the skin and seeds, then cut the peppers into slices. Leave to one side.

Meanwhile, mix together the cumin, coriander, garlic and lime juice in a large, non-metallic dish. Season to taste with salt and pepper. Add the fish and prawns and turn to coat them in the marinade. Leave to marinate, covered, in the fridge for 30 minutes.

Cook the potatoes in a pan of boiling salted water for 10–15 minutes until tender. Drain and leave the potatoes to one side.

Heat the olive oil in a large flameproof casserole or saucepan over a medium heat. Cook the onion, covered, for 8 minutes until softened. Add the ginger and thyme and cook for another minute. Pour in the chopped tomatoes and stock and bring to the boil. Stir in the harissa, then turn the heat down and simmer for 10 minutes until reduced, stirring occasionally.

Remove the fish and prawns from the marinade and stir the marinade into the casserole with the roast peppers, potatoes and olives. Gently stir in the fish, cover and cook for 8 minutes, then put the prawns on top and cook for another 3–4 minutes until pink and cooked through. Serve with couscous, with coriander scattered over and wedges of lime for squeezing over.

Butternut & Ginger Curd

It may sound unusual to use butternut squash in a sweet preserve, but this is sublime and has just the right amount of ginger to give a little zing without being overpowering. The squash also gives the curd the most vibrant golden colour.

MAKES 3 X 250G/9OZ JARS   PREPARATION TIME: 15 MINUTES   COOKING TIME: 40 MINUTES

1 small butternut squash, peeled, deseeded and chopped (about 600g/1lb 5oz prepared weight)
finely grated zest and juice of 1 lemon and 1 orange
75g/2½oz unsalted butter, cubed
200g/7oz/scant 1 cup granulated sugar
2 large eggs, plus 2 yolks, lightly beaten and strained
4 pieces stem ginger in syrup, diced, plus 3 tbsp of the syrup

Put the squash in a pan with 125ml/4fl oz/½ cup water and bring to the boil, then turn the heat down and simmer for 10 minutes, or until tender. Drain well and leave the squash in the colander to dry. Pass the squash through a sieve to make a smooth purée and discard any fibres left in the sieve.

Weigh 320g/11¼oz of the squash purée and put it in a heatproof bowl. Add the citrus zest and juice, butter, sugar and eggs and mix together. Put the bowl over a pan of gently simmering water, making sure the bottom doesn't touch the water. Heat the mixture to 85°C/185°F, stirring regularly, until the butter has melted, the sugar dissolves and the mixture thickens to a curd consistency. This will take 25–30 minutes. Take care you don't overheat the mixture as you don't want the eggs to scramble.

Stir the stem ginger and syrup into the curd and pour into sterilized jars, cover with lids and leave to cool. It will keep for 2 weeks stored in the fridge.

BUTTERNUT & GINGER CURD
PECORINO PASTA PARCELS

This recipe is a delicious twist on the classic pumpkin-filled pasta. The round parcels are served with a simple butter and sage sauce and finished off with a sprinkling of grated pecorino. Use "00" flour, which is extra fine and always recommended when making fresh pasta. You could swap the Butternut & Ginger Curd with mashed roasted butternut squash mixed with 1 teaspoon of finely chopped rosemary. When serving, spoon the pasta onto serving plates and then top with the sauce, rather than tipping the pasta into the sauce.

SERVES 4   PREPARATION TIME: 40 MINUTES, PLUS RESTING   COOKING TIME: 15 MINUTES

280g/10oz/2¼ cups "00" flour, plus extra
   for dusting
½ teaspoon salt
2 eggs, plus 2 yolks
fine semolina, for dusting
100g/3½ oz butter
2–3 tbsp chopped sage leaves, to taste

FILLING:
6 tablespoons Butternut & Ginger Curd
   (see page 156)
5 tbsp ground almonds
6 tbsp fresh white breadcrumbs
4 tbsp finely grated pecorino cheese,
   plus extra to serve
2 tbsp ricotta cheese
sea salt and freshly ground black pepper

To make the pasta, sift the flour into a large mixing bowl. Mix in the salt and make a well in the centre. Lightly beat the eggs and egg yolks together in a separate bowl and add half the beaten eggs to the flour. Mix the eggs into the dough using your fingers, adding the remaining egg when needed, until the mixture comes together to make a ball of dough.

Lightly dust a work surface with flour and knead the pasta dough for 3 minutes or until smooth, silky and elastic. Wrap the dough in cling film and leave to rest for at least 30 minutes in the fridge. (It will keep for up to 1 day in the fridge.)

Meanwhile, mix together all the ingredients for the filling. Season to taste with salt and pepper. Cover with cling film and leave in the fridge until ready to use.

Line two baking sheets with baking paper and sprinkle with semolina. Dust the work surface with flour again. Cut the ball of dough in half and wrap one half in the cling film to prevent it drying out.

Take a piece of dough, flatten it slightly and pass it through the widest setting of a pasta machine. Fold the dough over and pass it through again on the same setting. Repeat this process six times until you have a rectangular piece of dough. This will help to knead the dough, work the gluten and give it an al dente texture when cooked. Repeat with the second piece of dough, then wrap in cling film again.

To roll out the pasta, start with the pasta machine at its widest setting and pass the dough through the rollers. Repeat this process, passing the dough twice through each setting before turning it down by a grade.

CONTINUED ON PAGE **158**

Lightly dust the dough in flour if it is a little sticky and cut it in half crossways if it becomes too long to manage. Make sure you cover the rolled out dough with a dry, clean kitchen towel to prevent it drying out.

After passing the dough through the final setting, lay the fine sheet of pasta on the floured work surface. Using a 5.5cm/2¼ in round cutter, mark out circles where the parcels will be; don't cut through the pasta at this point.

Put a teaspoon of the filling in the centre of each circle, then lightly brush around the filling with water. Lay a second sheet of pasta on top, pressing around each lump of filling and squeezing out any air bubbles.

Press the cutter over again to cut out each parcel and seal the edges. To avoid a thick-edged parcel, press the edges together, pinching the dough all the way around the filling. Put the parcels on the prepared baking sheets and repeat until you have used all the dough and filling. The mixture will make about 40 parcels.

Cook the parcels in four batches in a large saucepan of boiling salted water for about 3 minutes, or until the pasta is al dente. Scoop the parcels out using a flat slotted spoon and keep warm in two covered shallow bowls in a low oven.

Meanwhile, melt the butter in a large frying pan, add the sage and heat through for 1 minute. Stir in 6 tablespoons of the pasta cooking water and season to taste with salt and pepper. Serve the pasta in large shallow bowls, coated in the butter sauce and sprinkled with extra pecorino.

Fresh Pasta

Making fresh egg pasta is immensely satisfying. All you need is a pasta machine (and even that isn't always necessary), the right type of flour and decent eggs. Tipo "00" is an extra fine flour that's traditionally used for egg pasta. It's sometimes combined with semolina, which gives the pasta extra "bite". The amount of added semolina differs depending on personal preference, as does the quantity of egg, which gives the pasta a silky richness.

When cooking pasta, the Italians often say "pasta likes friends", which means you have to keep an eye on it. Covering the pasta with plenty of water at a rolling boil is a must, and the water is meant to be as "salty as the sea". Don't overcrowd the pan as the pasta may stick together – there should be enough water to allow the pasta to bobble about. Egg pasta is traditionally served in the north of Italy with buttery, creamy sauces.

MUSHROOM PÂTÉ EN CROÛTE WITH RED ONION RELISH

This relish is particularly good with pâté, cheeses and meats, hot and cold, and is a real favourite on my home-made pizzas. The mushroom pâté, wrapped in puff pastry, can be served as a vegetarian Sunday lunch or as part of a picnic – either way don't forget a spoonful of onion relish.

SERVES 6   PREPARATION TIME: 30 MINUTES, PLUS SOAKING   COOKING TIME: 1 HOUR

25g/1oz dried porcini mushrooms
55g/2oz cashew nuts
1 tbsp olive oil
1 onion, finely chopped
3 cloves garlic, chopped
250g/9oz chestnut mushrooms, chopped
2 tsp dried thyme
5 tbsp fresh breadcrumbs
2 tbsp dark soy sauce
1 carrot, finely grated
325g/11½ oz ready-rolled puff pastry
flour, for dusting

1 small egg, lightly beaten
sea salt and freshly ground black pepper

RED ONION RELISH:
1kg/2lb 4oz red onions, thinly sliced
200ml/7fl oz/scant 1 cup red wine vinegar
2 cloves
½ tsp ground cinnamon
300g/10½ oz/scant 1⅔ cups soft light
   brown sugar
2 tbsp lemon juice

Pour just enough hot water over the porcini to cover and leave for 20 minutes until softened. Toast the cashews in a large dry frying pan for 3–5 minutes, turning once, until pale golden. Leave to cool.

Heat the olive oil in a large frying pan and cook the onion, covered, for 5 minutes until softened. Add the garlic, mushrooms and thyme and cook for another 5 minutes, stirring regularly, until tender. Drain the porcini, reserving 4 tablespoons of the soaking liquor, squeeze out any excess water then roughly chop. Add the porcini to the pan, stir and cook for another 5 minutes. Transfer the filling mixture to a bowl.

Preheat the oven to 200°C/400°F/Gas 6. Grind the toasted cashews in a food processor until finely chopped, then tip them into the bowl containing the mushroom mixture. Stir in the breadcrumbs, reserved soaking liquor, soy sauce and carrot until the mixture achieves a coarse pâté consistency. Season to taste.

Lay the pastry on a lightly floured work surface and spoon the mixture into a sausage shape down the centre. Draw up both sides of the pastry, trim any excess and wet the edges. Crimp to seal and make a seam down the centre of the parcel and use any spare pastry to decorate. Brush with egg, prick the top a few times with a fork. Transfer to a baking sheet and bake for 40–45 minutes until the pastry is golden and cooked through.

For the relish, put the onions, vinegar and spices in a non-reactive saucepan. Bring to the boil, turn the heat down and simmer, covered, for 20–30 minutes, stirring occasionally, until the onions are soft. Stir in the sugar and lemon juice, return to the boil, turn the heat down and simmer until thickened to a jam consistency. Remove and spoon into sterilized jars, cover with lids and cool. The relish will keep for 6 months. Store in a cool, dark place and put in the fridge once opened. Serve the pâté in slices with a good spoonful of the relish.

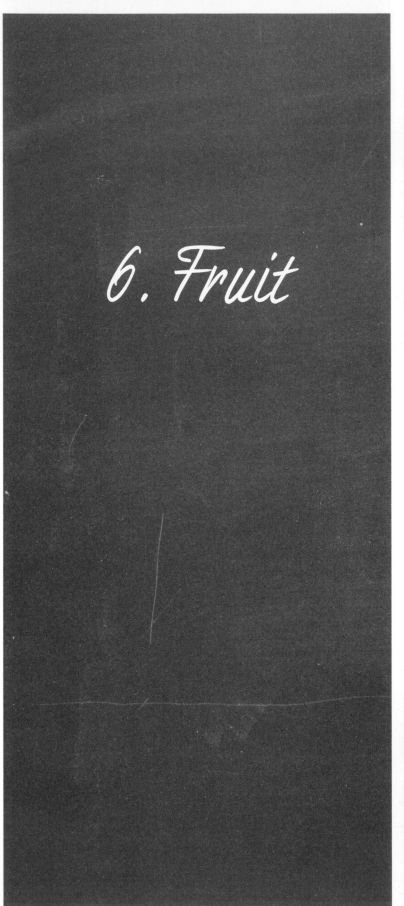

6. Fruit

MOROCCAN CHICKEN PATTIES WITH DATE CONFIT

These spiced chicken patties are wrapped in a Little Gem lettuce leaf with red onion and coriander and topped with a spoonful of sweet chilli-hot confit. Serve as a light meal with couscous and salad or as a canapé.

SERVES 4   PREPARATION TIME: 25 MINUTES, PLUS SOAKING   COOKING TIME: 50 MINUTES

600g/1lb 5oz skinless, boneless chicken breasts
4 garlic cloves, finely chopped
2.5cm/1in piece of fresh root ginger, peeled and grated
2 tsp ras el hanout
3 tbsp olive oil
½ tsp soft light brown sugar

TO SERVE:
16 small Little Gem lettuce leaves
10cm/4in piece cucumber, quartered lengthways, deseeded and diced

1 small red onion, diced
1 handful of coriander leaves

DATE CONFIT:
100g/3½ oz/heaped ½ cup ready-to-eat pitted dates, halved
1 tbsp olive oil
2 shallots, about 150g/5½ oz total weight, chopped
½ tsp ground cinnamon
1 bird's eye chilli, finely chopped
1 tsp soft light brown sugar
2 tbsp pomegranate molasses
sea salt and freshly ground black pepper

First make the date confit. Put the dates in a bowl, cover with just-boiled water and leave to soften for 1 hour. Meanwhile, heat the olive oil in a frying pan and fry the shallots, covered, for 20–25 minutes until very soft.

Drain the dates and add them to the pan, squashing them with the back of a fork to break them down. Stir in 4 tablespoons water, the cinnamon, chilli and sugar and cook for a further 5 minutes until it forms a thick jam consistency. Add more water if it is too thick. Stir in the pomegranate molasses and season with salt and pepper. You can blend the mixture if you prefer a smoother consistency. Spoon the mixture into a serving bowl and leave to cool.

Mince the chicken in a food processor and stir in the garlic, ginger and ras el hanout. Season with salt and pepper and then form the chicken mixture into 16 golf-ball-sized rounds. Flatten the top of each one to make a patty.

Heat two-thirds of the oil in a large, non-stick frying pan over a medium heat. Fry the patties in two or three batches for 3 minutes on each side. Just before they are cooked, sprinkle each side with a little sugar and fry briefly until slightly caramelized. Drain on kitchen paper and keep warm while you cook the remaining patties, adding more oil when necessary.

To serve, put a chicken patty on top of each lettuce leaf, scatter a little cucumber, red onion and coriander over and top with a spoonful of the date confit. Serve warm or at room temperature.

Raspberry Vinegar

This fruit-infused ruby-red vinegar is so versatile – add it to dressings, use it to deglaze a pan after browning meat, or pour it into sparkling mineral water to make a refreshing drink. Soups and stews also benefit from a splash of this sweet-sour condiment. Flavoured vinegars require a minimum of effort to prepare, yet a bottle makes an indispensable addition to the cook's repertoire of ingredients.

MAKES 2 X 250ML/9FL OZ/1 CUP BOTTLES   PREPARATION TIME: 10 MINUTES, PLUS 3 DAYS MACERATING AND AT LEAST 1 WEEK MATURING   COOKING TIME: 5 MINUTES

455ml/16fl oz/scant 2 cups white wine vinegar
115g/4oz/½ cup caster sugar
250g/9oz raspberries

Bring the vinegar to the boil in a non-reactive pan and allow to bubble away for 2 minutes. Remove from the heat and stir in the sugar until dissolved. Transfer to a heatproof bowl and leave to cool to 40°C/105°F.

Add the raspberries to the bowl and stir well, crushing the fruit slightly with the back of a fork. Cover and leave in a cool place to macerate for 3 days, stirring occasionally.

After 3 days, strain the vinegar through a jelly bag or muslin into a jug, then pour into sterilized bottles. Cover with lids and leave for at least a week before use. It will keep up to 6 months stored in a cool, dark place.

LAMB, BEETROOT & PUY LENTIL SALAD WITH **RASPBERRY VINEGAR** DRESSING

The combined qualities of a slightly syrupy texture and a fruity flavour mean that the raspberry vinegar is not only excellent in the dressing, but also works as a glaze for the lamb. If you aren't making your own raspberry vinegar, try to buy a good-quality ready-made one.

SERVES 4   PREPARATION TIME: 20 MINUTES, PLUS RESTING   COOKING TIME: 35 MINUTES

175g/6oz/heaped ¾ cup dried Puy lentils
1 tbsp concentrated chicken stock
4 thick lamb steaks, about 175g/6oz each
1 tbsp olive oil
1 tbsp Raspberry Vinegar (see page 164)
4 handfuls of baby spinach leaves
350g/12oz cooked beetroot in natural
    juice, drained and cubed
2 spring onions, finely sliced
1 long celery stick, thinly sliced
3 tbsp chopped parsley leaves

RASPBERRY VINEGAR DRESSING:
3 tbsp extra virgin olive oil
2 tbsp Raspberry Vinegar (see page 164)
1 heaped tsp clear honey
1 tsp Dijon mustard
sea salt and freshly ground black pepper

Cover the lentils with 2cm/¾in water and bring to the boil. Add the chicken stock, stir well, then turn the heat down and simmer part-covered for 30 minutes, or until tender, then drain.

Meanwhile, make the raspberry vinegar dressing. Put all the ingredients in a screw-top jar and shake until combined. Season to taste with salt and pepper.

Brush both sides of the lamb with the olive oil and season. Heat a large frying pan over a high heat and sear the lamb for 2 minutes on each side until golden. Turn the heat down to medium, pour over the vinegar and turn the lamb briefly until it is coated in the vinegar, oil and pan juices but remains pink in the centre. Remove the lamb from the pan and put it on a warm plate. Cover with foil and leave to rest for 10 minutes.

Put a handful of spinach on each serving plate and top with the lentils, beetroot, spring onions and celery. Cut the lamb into slices and put on the salad. Spoon the dressing over, toss lightly to combine, then scatter over the parsley before serving.

Preserved Lemons

If you haven't cooked with preserved lemons before, they are fantastic for sprucing up casseroles with a Middle Eastern or North African slant, mixing into a rub or stuffing for meat and fish, or adding to dressings. They have an intense salty, citrus flavour so use in moderate amounts.

**MAKES: 350G/12OZ JAR PREPARATION TIME: 20 MINUTES, PLUS 2 WEEKS INFUSING
COOKING TIME: 5 MINUTES**

170ml/5½ fl oz/⅔ cup white wine vinegar
60g/2¼ oz/¼ cup salt
50g/1¾ oz/scant ¼ cup granulated sugar
6 unwaxed lemons
½ tsp yellow mustard seeds
½ tsp coriander seeds
2 long red chillies

Put the vinegar, salt, sugar and 3 tablespoons water in a non-reactive pan. Bring to the boil and stir until the salt and sugar have dissolved. Boil for another minute, remove the pan from the heat and leave to cool.

Squeeze 2 of the lemons and add the juice to the cooling mixture. Slice the remaining lemons into 5mm/¼ in thick rounds, discarding the ends.

Use the best slices and put 4 around the sides of the sterilized jar, making sure they fit tightly together. Cut the remaining lemon slices into quarters. Put them in a bowl and then stir in the mustard and coriander seeds.

Pack the lemons and spices into the jar with the chillies. Add the liquid to cover the lemons. Cover and leave for 2 weeks before use. Store in a cool, dark place. When open, keep in the fridge. Use within 2 months.

PRESERVED LEMON-STUFFED SARDINES WITH GARLIC YOGURT SAUCE

Finely chopped preserved lemon is combined with herbs, spices and breadcrumbs to make a fragrant stuffing for fresh sardines. Mackerel and herrings would both make suitable alternatives to the sardines.

SERVES 4   PREPARATION TIME: 15 MINUTES   COOKING TIME: 18 MINUTES

olive oil, for greasing and drizzling
8–12 sardines, depending on their size, gutted, headed and descaled
watercress salad and crusty bread, to serve

PRESERVED LEMON STUFFING:
40g/1½ oz fresh white breadcrumbs
55g/2oz Preserved Lemons, finely chopped (see page 166). If using ready-prepared ones, scrape away and discard the flesh and finely chop the skin
1 tsp paprika

1 tsp ground coriander
½ red chilli, deseeded and finely chopped
2 tbsp olive oil
1 small handful of parsley leaves, chopped
1 small handful of mint leaves, chopped
sea salt and freshly ground black pepper

GARLIC YOGURT SAUCE:
150ml/5fl oz/scant ⅔ cup natural yogurt
1 garlic clove, crushed
juice of ½ lemon
2 tbsp chopped mint leaves

Preheat the oven to 200°C/400°F/Gas 6 and lightly oil a baking dish. Rinse the sardines inside and out, then pat dry with kitchen paper. Mix together all the ingredients for the stuffing and season to taste with salt and pepper.

Using a teaspoon, spoon the stuffing into the sardines, pressing it into the cavity of each fish.

Put the sardines in the prepared baking dish, drizzle with a little more olive oil and season with salt and pepper. Bake for 16–18 minutes until the sardines are cooked and the stuffing heated through.

Meanwhile, make the garlic yogurt sauce. Mix together the yogurt, garlic and lemon juice in a serving bowl, then season and scatter the mint over the top.

Serve the sardines with the yogurt sauce, a watercress salad and crusty bread.

DUCK WITH CHERRY & FIVE-SPICE SAUCE

Frozen cherries are perfect for this Chinese-spiced sauce as they break down when cooked into a rich, dark sauce, and they conveniently come ready pitted. Look for the dark, juicy morello cherries and you needn't bother defrosting them before cooking.

SERVES 4   PREPARATION TIME: 15 MINUTES   COOKING TIME: 35 MINUTES

a splash of olive oil
4 duck breasts, skin on
jasmine rice and finely chopped spring
   onions, to serve

CHERRY AND FIVE-SPICE SAUCE:
1 tbsp olive oil
1 shallot, diced
2.5cm/1in piece of fresh root ginger,
   peeled and grated

250g/9oz frozen dark cherries, preferably
   morello
1 tsp Chinese five-spice powder
finely grated zest and juice of 1 small
   orange
1 tbsp lemon juice
1 tsp cornflour
sea salt and freshly ground black pepper

To make the sauce, heat the olive oil in a saucepan over a medium heat and fry the shallot for 5 minutes until softened. Add the ginger and cook for another minute, then add the cherries, Chinese five-spice, orange zest and juice and lemon juice. Bring to the boil, then turn the heat down and simmer for 8 minutes until the cherries soften and start to break down.

Mix the cornflour with a little water, stir into the sauce and cook for another 5 minutes until reduced and thickened. Season with salt and pepper to taste and leave to cool slightly. Blend the sauce with a stick blender or mash depending on whether you prefer a smooth or slightly chunky sauce.

Meanwhile, preheat the oven to 190°C/375°F/Gas 5. Heat a splash of oil in a large, non-stick frying pan over a high heat. Put the duck breasts in the pan, skin-side down, and sear for 4 minutes until the skin is crisp. Transfer to a roasting tin, skin-side up, and roast for 8–10 minutes until cooked but still pink in the centre.

Slice the duck and serve with jasmine rice, sprinkled with spring onions and a good spoonful of the sauce. Any remaining sauce will keep in a sterilized jar for up to 2 weeks in the fridge.

> **"** *Fruit Sauces* **"**
>
> *I'm all for using fruit in savoury dishes, especially as the base of a sauce, but it's best to stick to classic combinations. Fruits that have a slight acidity work best in savoury dishes, such as cherries, apples, blackberries, blueberries, citrus fruit, rhubarb and even raspberries, helping to cut through the richness of meat, poultry and game.*

Orange, Coriander & Thyme Jam

In contrast to the slight bitterness of a marmalade made with Seville oranges (delicious as it is), this orange jam has a fresher, sweeter, citrusy flavour. It is infused with fresh thyme and the slightly lemony tang of coriander seeds. To make ginger jam, you can replace the thyme with two pieces of drained, finely chopped preserved ginger in syrup.

MAKES 2 X 300ML/10½FL OZ JARS   PREPARATION TIME: 15 MINUTES, PLUS OVERNIGHT SOAKING   COOKING TIME: 2 HOURS

3 tbsp coriander seeds
1kg/2lb 4oz unwaxed oranges, such as Valencia or Navel, washed and cut in half
2 lemons, washed and cut in half
875g/1lb 15oz/4 cups granulated sugar
4 tbsp thyme leaves

Toast the coriander seeds in a dry frying pan over a medium heat for about 3 minutes, or until they start to smell aromatic. Leave to cool, then roughly crush using a pestle and mortar. Leave to one side.

Squeeze the orange and lemon juice into a large bowl and strain, reserving the sieve contents. Using a spoon, scrape out the pith and membrane from the skins into a bowl, then add the sieve contents.

Thinly slice the skin from 2 of the oranges and add it to the juice. Roughly chop the remaining orange skin and add to the bowl with the pips. Tip the pips, membrane, lemon skin and roughly chopped orange skin into the centre of a large square of muslin. Scatter the toasted coriander seeds over and twist the muslin and tie a knot in the top to make a bag.

Pour the juice into a preserving or stainless steel saucepan with 1.75l/60fl oz/6⅔ cups water. Add the muslin bag, pressing it down to submerge it in the liquid, then leave, covered, overnight.

The next day, bring the liquid in the pan to the boil, then turn the heat down and simmer for 1½ hours until the peel is really soft and the liquid has reduced by half. Squeeze out any liquid from the bag of pips, then remove and discard the bag.

Add the sugar and stir until dissolved. Increase the heat and bring the mixture to a rapid, rolling boil for 15 minutes, or until setting point is reached. Test for a set, either with a sugar thermometer (it should read 110°C/225°F), or put a teaspoonful of the orange jam onto a cold saucer and leave it to cool for a few minutes. If it wrinkles when you push it with your finger, then it is ready. Stir the thyme into the jam and carefully spoon it into sterilized jars. Cover with lids and leave to cool.

ROAST GUINEA FOWL GLAZED WITH
ORANGE, CORIANDER & THYME JAM

The fresh, citrusy flavour of the jam is great with guinea fowl, giving the skin a wonderful golden glaze and imparting a delicious sweetness to the resulting gravy.

SERVES 4   PREPARATION TIME: 25 MINUTES   COOKING TIME: 1 HOUR 35 MINUTES

1.7kg/3lb 12oz guinea fowl
2 tbsp Orange, Coriander & Thyme Jam
   (see page 170)
1 large parsnip
6 tbsp sunflower oil
300ml/10½ fl oz/scant 1¼ cups
   good-quality chicken stock

LEMON AND HERB STUFFING
40g/1½ oz butter
1 onion, finely chopped
75g/2½ oz/heaped 1 cup fresh white
   breadcrumbs
1 tbsp thyme leaves
1 tbsp chopped flat-leaf parsley
finely grated zest of 1 lemon
salt and freshly ground black pepper

Preheat the oven to 180°C/350°F/Gas 4. Wash and pat the guinea fowl dry with kitchen paper. Leave to one side while you make the stuffing.

Melt the butter in a frying pan over a gentle heat and fry the onion for 8 minutes, stirring occasionally, until softened. Remove from the heat and stir in the breadcrumbs, herbs and lemon zest, then season with salt and pepper.

Loosely stuff the guinea fowl with the lemon and herb stuffing, then put it on a rack over a roasting tin filled with about 2.5cm/1in water. Using your hands, smear the jam all over the guinea fowl until it is completely covered. Tie the legs together with a piece of string and roast for 1¼ hours, basting with the juices in the tin halfway through. Test the bird is ready by inserting a skewer into the thickest part of the leg – the juices should run clear. If not, return the guinea fowl to the oven for another 10 minutes.

Meanwhile, using a vegetable peeler, slice the parsnip into long, thin strips. Heat the sunflower oil in a frying pan over a medium-high heat and fry the parsnip in two or three batches for a few minutes until the strips are crisp and golden. Drain on kitchen paper.

Put the guinea fowl on a warm plate, cover loosely with foil and leave to rest while you make the gravy.

Spoon off any surplus fat from the tin, then add the stock and bring to the boil over a hob, stirring to remove any bits stuck to the bottom and sides of the tin. Season to taste, and cook until reduced and thickened. Carve the guinea fowl and serve with the stuffing, gravy and parsnip crisps.

SLOW-COOKED PORK WITH APPLES & CIDER SAUCE

Instead of serving the pork roasted in the conventional way, the joint in this recipe is cooked long and slow in a fruity cider sauce. A spoonful of redcurrant jelly adds just the right amount of sweetness and colour to the dish.

SERVES 4–6   PREPARATION TIME: 20 MINUTES   COOKING TIME: 3½ HOURS

- 1.1kg/2lb 7oz boneless pork leg or shoulder joint, skin scored
- 1 tbsp olive oil
- 2 onions, thickly sliced
- 1 carrot, thickly sliced
- 4 garlic cloves, sliced
- 2 rosemary sprigs, leaves removed
- 1 bay leaf
- 300ml/10½ fl oz/scant 1¼ cups dry cider
- 200ml/7fl oz/scant 1 cup good-quality chicken stock
- 2 apples, cored and cut into 8 wedges
- 2 tsp redcurrant jelly
- 10g/¼ oz butter, softened
- 2 tsp plain flour
- sea salt and freshly ground black pepper

Preheat the oven to 170°C/325°F/Gas 3. To make crackling, cut off the skin and adjoining fat from the pork joint. Put it in a dish and pour over just-boiled water; this will help to open out the cuts in the skin. Drain well, pat dry, and season generously with salt and pepper. Leave to one side until ready to cook.

Heat the olive oil in a large flameproof casserole and brown the pork for 2 minutes on each side until coloured all over. Remove from the pan and leave to one side.

Add the onions and carrot to the pan and cook for 3 minutes, then stir in the garlic, rosemary and bay leaf. Return the pork to the casserole and pour in the cider and chicken stock. Bring to the boil, cover with a lid and transfer the casserole to the oven. Cook for 2¼ hours, then remove from the oven and add the apples around the pork. Return to the oven for 45 minutes. At the same time put the pork skin in the oven and cook for 1 hour until crisp and golden.

Remove the pork and apples from the casserole, transfer them to a warm plate, cover with foil and leave to rest while you make the sauce. Turn up the oven to 220°C/425°F/Gas 7 to crisp up the crackling while the pork is resting.

Skim the fat from the surface of the cooking liquid in the casserole, then strain it through a sieve into a saucepan, pressing the vegetables to remove as much liquid as possible. Stir in the redcurrant jelly and bring to the boil. Cook for 10 minutes or until the sauce has reduced by half.

Meanwhile, mix together the butter and flour to make a paste. Reduce the heat to low and stir the paste into the sauce, a little at a time. Season to taste with salt and pepper, then simmer until thickened. Slice the pork and crackling and serve with the sauce spooned over and the roasted apples on the side.

Lemon Curd

One of my favourite desserts is home-made lemon meringue pie, so when I developed this recipe the aim was to create a curd that would double up as a pie or cake filling as well as make a delicious preserve. The result is a curd with a really gutsy, zingy lemon flavour combined with a rich, creamy texture – it's always a big hit with the family!

MAKES 3 X 175G/6OZ JARS   PREPARATION TIME: 10 MINUTES   COOKING TIME: 15 MINUTES

finely grated zest of 1 lemon
juice of 3 lemons
165g/5¾oz butter
260g/9¼oz/scant 1¼ cups granulated sugar
4 eggs

Put the lemon zest and juice in a non-reactive pan with the butter and sugar. Stir and warm over a low heat, stirring until the butter has melted and the sugar dissolves, then remove from the heat.

Whisk the eggs using a stick blender until combined, then whisk them into the butter mixture. Return the pan to a low heat and cook for about 5 minutes, stirring continuously with a wooden spoon, or until the mixture thickens to a custard consistency and any white foam on the top disappears. Make sure the mixture does not boil as the eggs can curdle.

Remove the pan from the heat and pour the curd into sterilized jars and cover with lids. To sterilize the space between the lid and the lemon curd, wrap each jar carefully in a kitchen towel and turn it upside down for 2 seconds and back. Leave to cool, then store in the fridge. The curd will keep for up to 2 weeks.

LEMON CURD MERINGUE SEMIFREDDO

This takes all my favourite bits from a lemon meringue pie and transforms them into a deliciously indulgent creamy dessert. Semifreddo is not quite an ice cream as you don't have to churn it, but it's equally good and, as its name suggests, it's semi-frozen so you can take it out of the freezer just before serving. You won't need all of the meringues – save these for another day served with softly whipped cream – but you could use ready-made ones.

**SERVES 8–10   PREPARATION TIME: 30 MINUTES, PLUS FREEZING
COOKING TIME: 1¼ HOURS**

2 large eggs, separated
125g/4½ oz/heaped ½ cup caster sugar
grated zest of 1 large lemon, plus extra
   to serve
125ml/4fl oz/½ cup Lemon Curd
   (see page 176)
300ml/10½ fl oz/scant 1¼ cups double
   cream

MERINGUES (MAKES 8):
2 large egg whites at room temperature
60g/2¼ oz/¼ cup caster sugar
60g/2¼ oz/½ cup icing sugar

Preheat the oven to 110°C/225°F/Gas ½, and line two baking sheets with baking paper. To make the meringues, use an electric hand whisk on a medium speed, whisk the egg whites in a large, grease-free mixing bowl until they form stiff peaks. Turn the speed up and gradually add the caster sugar. Continue whisking between each addition.

Sift half of the icing sugar into the bowl and gently fold it into the egg whites with a metal spoon. Add the remaining icing sugar and fold it in without over-mixing and losing the air. The mixture should look glossy, smooth and light.

Take a heaped dessertspoon of the meringue mixture and ease it onto the prepared baking sheet into a round. Repeat with the remaining mixture to make 8 rounds. Bake for 1–1¼ hours until the meringues are risen and sound hollow when tapped underneath. Leave to cool on a wire rack.

Line the base and sides of a 900g/2lb loaf tin with a double layer of cling film, leaving a generous overhang.

Whisk the egg yolks and sugar in a large mixing bowl until pale and fluffy. Fold in the lemon zest and curd. In a second bowl, whip the cream until it forms soft peaks, then gently fold this into the egg yolk mixture.

In a clean mixing bowl and using a clean whisk, whisk the egg whites until they form stiff peaks. Gently fold them into the egg yolk mixture. Spoon half of the semifreddo mixture into the prepared loaf tin. Break 2 of the meringues into fairly chunky pieces and scatter them over, then top with the remaining semifreddo mixture. Cover the top with the excess hanging cling film and freeze for about 5 hours or until firm.

Once set, turn the semifreddo out onto a serving plate and remove the cling film. Crumble 2 more of the meringues over the top and sprinkle with a little lemon zest. Serve cut into slices.

POACHED PEACHES IN LEMONGRASS & GINGER SYRUP

Peaches, nectarines, pears, plums and cherries, in fact any slightly firm fruit, can be poached. It's best to use just-ripe or even slightly under-ripe fruit since if it is too soft there is a danger the fruit will not hold its shape when poached. Here, the peaches are poached in a ginger- and lemongrass-infused syrup, but you could substitute half the water with white rum or rosé wine.

**SERVES 4   PREPARATION TIME: 10 MINUTES, PLUS COOLING AND CHILLING
COOKING TIME: 25 MINUTES**

100g/3½ oz/scant ½ cup caster sugar
4 tbsp clear honey
1 lemongrass stalk, outer layer removed
  and bruised with the blade of a knife

5cm/2in piece of fresh root ginger, peeled
  and sliced into rounds
juice of ½ lemon
6 just-ripe peaches, halved and stoned

To make the poaching liquid, put 455ml/16fl oz/scant 2 cups water, the sugar, honey, lemongrass, ginger and lemon juice in a saucepan. Bring to the boil over a medium heat, stirring to dissolve the sugar. Turn the heat down to low and simmer for 5 minutes.

Add the peaches and poach, turning them every so often until tender; this will take about 8–10 minutes. Using a slotted spoon, remove the peaches and leave to one side until cool enough to handle.

Increase the heat under the pan and bring the poaching liquid to the boil, then bubble away until reduced; you should have about 300ml/10½fl oz/scant 1¼ cups light syrup. Leave to one side to cool, then remove and discard the lemongrass and ginger.

Carefully peel the peaches and put them in a serving bowl. Pour the syrup over the peaches and chill until ready to serve. They will keep for up to 2 days in the fridge.

Bottling Poached Fruit

To bottle poached fruit, use sterilized Kilner jars and a saucepan deep enough for the jars to be submerged in water without touching each other or the pan sides. Put a cloth in the base of the pan to keep the jars stable. The timing of the bottling depends on the fruit's acidity levels and the size of the jar, so check the recipe before you begin. After bottling, allow the jar to cool slowly. Check the seal by carefully picking up the jar by the lid – if it hasn't properly sealed, it should be refrigerated and eaten within a week. Store in a cool, dry, dark place for up to 6 months.

RHUBARB BURNT CREAM

Rhubarb and custard – is there a more delicious combination? The tartness of the fruit is perfect with the sweet, creamy custard, which is best made up to 1 day in advance.

**SERVES 4   PREPARATION TIME: 15 MINUTES, PLUS CHILLING AND SETTING
COOKING TIME: 45 MINUTES**

300ml/10½ fl oz/scant 1¼ cups
    double cream
1 vanilla pod, split lengthways
4 large egg yolks
2 tbsp caster sugar, plus extra for
    sprinkling

RHUBARB COMPÔTE:
200g/7oz rhubarb, cut into chunks
2 tbsp caster sugar
2 tbsp orange juice

Preheat the oven to 170°C/325°F/Gas 3. First make the rhubarb compôte. Mix the rhubarb, sugar and orange juice in a non-metallic pan. Bring to the boil, stirring to dissolve the sugar, then turn the heat down and simmer for 10–12 minutes until the rhubarb is tender and has broken down. Leave to cool.

Heat the cream in a pan with the vanilla pod until it almost comes to the boil.

Meanwhile, in a mixing bowl, whisk the egg yolks with the sugar until pale, then whisk in the hot cream. Strain the custard through a sieve into a jug. (Rinse the vanilla pod, dry well and insert into a jar of sugar to make vanilla sugar.)

Spoon the rhubarb into four 170ml/5½fl oz/⅔ cup ramekins. Pour the custard over the top until almost to the top of the ramekins. Put the ramekins in a roasting tin and pour in enough just-boiled water to come halfway up the sides. Bake for 20–25 minutes or until the top of the custard is just set. Remove from the oven and leave to cool. Cover with cling film and chill overnight (or a minimum of 2 hours, if you can't wait).

Preheat the grill to high. Sprinkle a thin layer of caster sugar over each custard and place under the hot grill until the sugar bubbles and starts to caramelize. You can use a blowtorch but take care either way as the sugar can easily burn. Leave the sugar to harden and cool slightly, then serve immediately.

Fruit Compôtes

Delicious for breakfast when mixed with thick natural yogurt or as a simple dessert, fruit compôtes are made of whole or pieces of fruit, which are cooked in a sugar syrup until they have softened and taken on a sticky sweetness. The fruit syrup can be flavoured with vanilla, cinnamon, cloves or strips of orange or lemon zest, among many other things.

Pineapple in Vanilla Rum

Preserving fruit in alcohol is one of the oldest and most delicious ways to extend the life of fresh fruit. It's worth experimenting with different types of fruit and alcohol – clementines in brandy, raspberries in vodka, figs in red wine, the options are endless...

MAKES 1L/35FL OZ/4 CUPS   PREPARATION TIME: 10 MINUTES
COOKING TIME: 20 MINUTES, PLUS COOLING AND 1 MONTH INFUSING

1 large, just-ripe pineapple
300g/10½ oz/scant 1⅓ cups caster sugar
1 cinnamon stick
1 vanilla pod
250ml/9fl oz/1 cup white rum

Stand the pineapple upright on a chopping board. Cut away the green top, the tough outer skin and the "eyes", then remove the core with a corer, if you have one. Alternatively remove the core after the pineapple is sliced. Cut the pineapple into rounds, then each slice into quarters.

Put 200ml/7fl oz/scant 1 cup water and half the sugar into a large, wide, shallow saucepan. Add the cinnamon and vanilla and simmer over a low heat, stirring until the sugar dissolves.

Add the pineapple to the sugar syrup and simmer over a low heat for 5 minutes, turning the fruit once.

Put a colander over a bowl and spoon the pineapple into it. Return any of the syrup that has dripped into the bowl to the pan and leave the pineapple to cool.

Add the remaining sugar to the poaching liquid and simmer, stirring until the sugar dissolves. Increase the heat and bring to the boil. Continue to boil the liquid until the temperature rises to 110°C/230°F on a sugar thermometer and it becomes syrupy. Carefully pour the syrup into a jug and leave to cool. Stir the rum into the cooled syrup until combined.

Spoon the cooled pineapple into a sterilized jar along with the vanilla pod; discard the cinnamon stick. Pour the rum syrup over to cover the fruit completely. Cover the jar with a lid and store in a cool, dark place for 1 month before using. It will keep for up to 6 months, but store in the fridge once opened and use within 1 month.

COCONUT & LIME BAKED CHEESECAKE WITH
PINEAPPLE IN VANILLA RUM

*There is nothing quite like a baked cheesecake and, while this American classic is delicious
served plain, this version is topped with whipped vanilla cream and rum-soaked pineapple.*

**SERVES 8–10   PREPARATION TIME: 25 MINUTES, PLUS COOLING
COOKING TIME: 1 HOUR 20 MINUTES**

butter, for greasing
250g/9oz/1 cup ricotta cheese
400g/14oz/heaped 1½ cups curd cheese
  or cream cheese
2 tsp vanilla extract
finely grated zest and juice of 1 lime
3 eggs
165g/5¾oz/scant ¾ cup caster sugar

TOPPING:
250ml/9fl oz/1 cup whipping cream
1 tsp vanilla extract

1 tbsp icing sugar
⅓ recipe quantity Pineapple
  in Vanilla Rum (see page 182),
  drained well
ground ginger and pared zest of 1 lime,
  cut into fine strips, to serve

BASE:
3 tbsp unsweetened desiccated coconut
125g/4½ oz gingernut biscuits, crushed
70g/2½ oz unsalted butter, melted

Preheat the oven to 150°C/300°F/Gas 2. Grease the sides of a deep 20cm/8in springform cake tin with
butter. Line the base with baking paper and grease again.

To make the cheesecake base, put the coconut in a large, non-stick frying pan and toast over a medium-low
heat for 3 minutes, stirring occasionally with a wooden spoon, until light golden. Put the coconut in a large
bowl and leave to cool.

When the coconut is cool, add the crushed biscuits and melted butter and stir well until combined. Tip the
mixture into the prepared tin and press down with the back of a spoon into a firm, even layer. Cover with
cling film and chill until needed.

Put the ricotta, curd cheese and vanilla extract in a blender and blend until smooth, then add the lime zest
and juice, eggs and sugar and blend again until combined.

Pour the ricotta and curd cheese mixture over the biscuit base and bake for 1¼ hours until set, but still
a little wobbly. Remove from the oven and leave to cool in the tin on a wire rack.

To make the topping, whip the cream, vanilla extract and icing sugar using an electric hand whisk until it
forms soft peaks. Transfer the cheesecake to a serving plate and spoon the whipped cream over the top.
Pile on the pineapple and sprinkle with a little ground ginger and lime zest before serving.

CHOCOLATE RISOTTO WITH BOOZY CHERRIES

A sweet risotto may sound unusual, but the short-grain Arborio is equally happy used in a rice pudding as it is in a savoury risotto. Serve the intensely chocolatey pudding in small bowls, topped with the cherries steeped in kirsch and a splash of cream, if you like.

SERVES 4–6   **PREPARATION TIME: 15 MINUTES, PLUS RESTING**   **COOKING TIME: 50 MINUTES**

875ml/30fl oz/3½ cups whole milk
60g/2¼ oz/¼ cup caster sugar
165g/5¾ oz/¾ cup Arborio rice
60g/2¼ oz dark chocolate, about 70%
   cocoa solids, cut into small pieces
1 tsp vanilla bean paste
single cream, to serve (optional)

BOOZY CHERRIES:
650g/1lb 7oz dark cherries
60g/2¼ oz/¼ cup caster sugar
3 tbsp kirsch or brandy
2 tsp cornflour

Preheat the oven to 150°C/300°F/Gas 2. Put the milk, sugar and rice into a flameproof casserole. Bring the milk almost to the boil, stirring occasionally with a wooden spoon. Add the chocolate and keep stirring until it melts.

Stir in the vanilla, cover with a lid and transfer to the oven. Bake for 40–45 minutes, stirring occasionally, until the rice is tender. Stir any skin that forms on the surface into the rice and leave it to rest, covered, for 5 minutes before serving.

Meanwhile, make the boozy cherries. Put the cherries, sugar and 2 tablespoons water in a saucepan and bring to a simmer, stirring until the sugar dissolves. Mix together the kirsch and cornflour and gradually stir the mixture into the cherries. Simmer for another 2–3 minutes until the sauce has thickened and the cherries are tender.

Serve the chocolate risotto topped with the cherries and a swirl of cream, if you like. Any spare boozy cherries can be transferred to a sterilized jar and covered with a lid. They will keep for 1 week stored in the fridge.

Preserving Fruit in Alcohol

Steeping in alcohol is one of the easiest ways to preserve fruit. To make a longer-lasting version of Boozy Cherries, follow the instructions on page 182 for Pineapple in Vanilla Rum using the same quantity of cherries as above, 300g/10½oz/scant 1⅓ cups caster sugar and 250ml/9fl oz/1 cup kirsch or brandy. You could also flavour the sugar syrup with 2 star anise. The cherries will keep for up to 6 months stored in a cool, dark place. Once opened, use within 1 month and store in the fridge.

EXOTIC CHRISTMAS PUDDING WITH COCONUT & RUM CREAM

The traditional British festive pudding is given a tropical twist with the addition of dried mango, spices, dark rum and dark chocolate. Don't be put off by the long list of ingredients as it's very easy to make. If you want to make the pudding in advance, leave it to cool after steaming, then replace the greaseproof paper and foil top with new discs and secure as before. Store in a cool, dark place for up to 2 months. To reheat, steam the pudding for 2 hours.

SERVES 6   PREPARATION TIME: 30 MINUTES, PLUS SOAKING   COOKING TIME: 3 HOURS

165g/5¾oz dried mango
85g/3oz/⅔ cup plain flour
4 tsp cocoa powder
100g/3½oz/1¾ cups fresh white breadcrumbs
1 tsp mixed spice
1 tsp ground cinnamon
1 tsp ground ginger
150g/5½oz/heaped ¾ cup dark muscovado sugar
150g/5½oz chilled butter, diced, plus extra for greasing
150g/5½oz pitted dates, chopped

150g/5½oz/scant 1¼ cups raisins
80g/2¾oz dark chocolate, about 70% cocoa solids, chopped
grated zest of 1 large orange
3 eggs, lightly beaten
5 tbsp dark rum, plus extra to serve

COCONUT AND RUM CREAM:
250ml/9fl oz/1 cup thick double cream
125ml/4fl oz/½ cup coconut cream
4 tbsp dark rum, plus extra for drizzling
3 tbsp icing sugar, or to taste

Put the mango in a bowl, cover with hot water and leave to soften for 1 hour. Drain well, then roughly chop the mango and leave to one side.

Sift the flour and cocoa powder into a large mixing bowl, then stir in the breadcrumbs, ground spices and sugar. Rub the butter into the mixture with your fingertips until it resembles coarse breadcrumbs. Stir in the chopped mango, dates, raisins, chocolate pieces and orange zest.

Mix together the beaten eggs and dark rum and pour over the fruit mixture, then stir well until combined. Lightly grease a 1.2l/40fl oz/4¾ cup pudding basin and fill with the mixture until 1cm/½in below the rim. Gently tap the basin on a work surface to release any air bubbles and level the top with the back of a spoon.

Cover the pudding with a disc of greaseproof paper and a double layer of foil, each with a pleat down the middle to allow the pudding to expand, then secure with string. Put the pudding on an upturned saucer in a large saucepan. Pour in enough boiling water to come halfway up the basin sides. Cover with a lid and steam for 3 hours until cooked and firm. Keep an eye on the water levels and replenish as necessary.

To make the coconut and rum cream, beat the double cream and coconut cream together in a bowl and fold in the rum and sugar, adding more to taste. Spoon the cream into a serving bowl and chill. Turn the pudding out onto a serving plate. Pour over a little rum and set alight. Serve with the coconut and rum cream.

RASPBERRY, AMARETTI & SALTED CARAMEL VERRINES

A verrine is a layered dessert that works best visually and flavour-wise when there are contrasting layers of colour and texture. The combination of crisp crunch from the amaretti biscuits; sticky, salty caramel sauce; thick whipped cream and slightly tart raspberries make these verrines a great success.

SERVES 4   PREPARATION TIME: 20 MINUTES   COOKING TIME: 8 MINUTES

400ml/14fl oz/generous 1½ cups
   double cream
1 tsp vanilla bean paste
4 tsp icing sugar
100g/3½ oz amaretti biscuits, roughly
   crumbled
250g/9oz/scant 1½ cups raspberries

SALTED CARAMEL SAUCE:
90g/3¼ oz unsalted butter
165g/5¾ oz/scant 1 cup soft light brown
   sugar
½ tsp vanilla bean paste
125ml/4floz/½ cup double cream
¼ tsp sea salt flakes

First make the salted caramel sauce. Melt the butter in a small saucepan over a medium-low heat. Add the sugar and stir until it dissolves. Add the vanilla and cream and bring to boiling point. Turn the heat down and simmer for 5 minutes, stirring continuously until thickened and the colour of toffee. Stir in the salt and leave to one side.

Using an electric hand whisk, whip the cream until it starts to thicken. Add the vanilla and sugar and continue to whisk until a soft peak consistency.

Crumble a quarter of the amaretti into each glass. Top with a layer of the salted caramel sauce, followed by a layer of cream and topped off with raspberries. Chill until ready to serve.

F. Bakes

OATCAKES

Perfect served with your favourite cheese, smoked salmon or charcuterie, these Scottish savoury biscuits are traditionally plain, but you could experiment with different flavourings. For herb biscuits, stir in ½–1 teaspoon of thyme, rosemary, sage or parsley. Spices such as cayenne pepper, smoked paprika, celery salt or mixed spice work well for a sweeter option. Grated mature Cheddar or sesame seeds are good, or you could sweeten the biscuits by stirring 1 teaspoon of caster sugar into the dry ingredients or adding finely chopped dried fruit.

MAKES 16   PREPARATION TIME: 10 MINUTES   COOKING TIME: 18 MINUTES

60g/2¼ oz/scant ½ cup wholemeal spelt or plain flour, plus extra for dusting
1 tsp bicarbonate of soda
½ tsp salt

140g/5oz/heaped 1 cup medium oatmeal, plus extra for dusting
60g/2¼ oz unsalted butter

Preheat the oven to 180°C/350°F/Gas 4 and line a baking sheet with baking paper.

Sift the flour, bicarbonate of soda and salt into a mixing bowl, then stir in the oatmeal. Rub in the butter with your fingertips until the mixture resembles coarse breadcrumbs. Stir in about 3 tablespoons water and bring the mixture together to make a dough. Knead lightly in a bowl to make a ball of dough.

Lightly dust a work surface with a mixture of flour and oatmeal. Roll out the dough on the prepared surface until about 4mm/⅛in thick and cut into 16 rounds using a 5.5cm/2¼in fluted cutter. Put on the prepared baking sheet and bake for 15–18 minutes until crisp. Leave to cool on a wire rack and store in an airtight container for up to 3 days.

Oatmeal

Oatmeal is made from cutting or grinding whole oats (groats) and is available in various grades. For these oatcakes, look for a medium-ground oatmeal, which gives them a slightly coarse texture and nutty flavour. If you prefer a finer, or indeed coarser-textured oatcake, feel free to adapt the oatmeal you use, but bear in mind that a dough made with coarse oatmeal will be more tricky to work with.

CHEESE & CAYENNE BISCUITS

These light, crumbly, cheesy biscuits always go down well with friends. They make the perfect nibble with drinks or a delicious savoury snack topped with a spoonful of a mild soft goat's cheese and a sun-blush tomato.

MAKES 20   PREPARATION TIME: 15 MINUTES, PLUS CHILLING   COOKING TIME: 15 MINUTES

165g/5¾oz/1⅓ cups plain flour, sifted,
   plus extra for dusting
1 tsp cayenne pepper

90g/3¼oz butter, cubed
90g/3¼oz mature Cheddar cheese,
   grated

Put the flour and half of the cayenne into a mixing bowl. Rub in the butter with your fingertips to make a soft, slightly crumbly mixture, then stir in the Cheddar. Form into a soft ball of dough and knead briefly in the bowl until the cheese is evenly distributed. Wrap the dough in cling film and chill for 30 minutes to firm up.

Line a large baking tray with baking paper. Roll out the dough on a lightly floured work surface into a long rectangle about 7cm/2¾in wide and 5mm/¼in thick. Cut into 2.5cm/1in wide fingers and arrange, spaced apart, on the lined baking tray. Chill for another 20 minutes to firm up. This will help the biscuits to keep their shape during baking.

Meanwhile, preheat the oven to 190°C/375°F/Gas 5. Sprinkle the biscuits with the remaining cayenne and bake for 12–15 minutes until golden and crisp. Leave to cool on a wire rack.

"SLEEPLESS" SPELT BREAD

This bread uses an overnight starter – hence the name – which not only improves the flavour, but gives it a good crust and extends its keeping qualities. I've used spelt flour, but you can use regular strong wheat flour, if preferred.

MAKES 2 LOAVES PREPARATION TIME: 20 MINUTES, PLUS OVERNIGHT RISING AND PROVING COOKING TIME: 30 MINUTES

1kg/2lb 4oz/8 cups white spelt flour, plus extra for dusting
5g/⅛oz easy blend dried yeast
1 heaped tbsp sea salt

vegetable oil, for greasing
1 egg, lightly beaten
1 tbsp whole oat flakes, for sprinkling (optional)

The day before you bake, mix together the flour, yeast and salt in a large mixing bowl. Using a fork and then your fingers, slowly mix in 580ml/20¼fl oz/2⅓ cups tepid water, adding enough to make a soft dough.

Knead on a lightly floured work surface for 10 minutes until the dough is smooth and elastic. Shape the dough into a ball for rising.

Put the dough in a clean, lightly oiled bowl and cover with cling film. Leave to rise at room temperature overnight, or for about 9 hours (the dough can be left up to 16 hours if necessary) until doubled in size.

The next day, knock back the dough by pressing the dough with your knuckles, then tip it out of the bowl onto a lightly floured work surface. Divide the dough into 2 and shape into rounds. Put the loaves on a floured baking tray, cover with a clean kitchen towel and leave to prove for 2–3 hours until almost doubled in size.

Preheat the oven to 220°C/425°F/Gas 7. Brush the top of each loaf with beaten egg and scatter the oat flakes over, if using. Bake for 25–30 minutes until golden and hollow sounding when tapped underneath.

Spelt Flour

Once widely grown in parts of Europe, spelt is undergoing a revival due in part to its traditional "what wheat used to taste like" flavour and the fact that it is generally more tolerated by those with a wheat intolerance. This ancient variety of wheat produces a pale greyish flour and has a slightly nutty flavour. It can be used to make bread as well as pastry, biscuits and cakes.

SOURDOUGH

Sourdough bread has become hugely popular, but the origins of this artisan, long-fermented, natural yeast bread goes way back. If you haven't made sourdough before it's a labour of love and requires time and patience, but it's hugely rewarding when you produce a magnificent air-textured, golden, crusty loaf – and it can become slightly addictive!

MAKES 1 LOAF   PREPARATION TIME: STARTER 5 DAYS; SPONGE 5 MINUTES PLUS OVERNIGHT STANDING; LOAF 25 MINUTES, PLUS RISING AND PROVING COOKING TIME: 40 MINUTES

STARTER:
300g/10½ oz/2⅓ cups strong white flour
   (divide into 5 x 60g/2¼ oz/½ cup
   batches)

SPONGE STARTER:
300g/10½ oz of the starter (keep the
   remaining starter for your next batch
   of bread. Cover with the lid of the
   Kilner jar and store in the fridge)
250g/9oz/2 cups strong white flour

DOUGH:
350g/12oz/heaped 2¾ cups strong white
   flour, plus extra for dusting
1 tbsp clear honey
1 tbsp sea salt
vegetable oil, for greasing

TO MAKE THE STARTER:
Day 1
Add 60ml/2fl oz/4 tbsp bottled spring or filtered water at room temperature and 60g/2¼ oz/½ cup organic spelt or strong white flour to a large Kilner jar. Stir well until combined, then cover with a clean kitchen towel. Leave at room temperature for 24 hours.

Day 2
Repeat Day 1.

Day 3
Repeat Day 1.

Day 4
Repeat Day 1.

Day 5
Repeat Day 1.

Day 6
The starter is now ready to use. You should have a lively, bubbly starter the consistency of thick paint and it should smell beery, sweet and slightly yeasty. This will develop with use and age.

TO MAKE THE SPONGE STARTER:

Put 300g/10½oz of the starter in a large bowl, add 300ml/10½fl oz/scant 1¼ cups tepid filtered water and the flour. Mix until combined, cover with cling film and leave to stand overnight at room temperature. The mixture will have increased in size and will look puffy and bubbly; now make the dough.

TO MAKE THE DOUGH:

Add the flour, honey and salt to the sponge starter. Mix well and cover with cling film and leave to stand for 20 minutes. Tip out onto a floured work surface and knead for 10–15 minutes. It will be quite soft and sticky at first but keep kneading until it becomes a smooth, elastic ball of dough. (If the dough is unmanageably wet before kneading, add extra flour, or, alternatively, if it is too dry add a splash more water.)

Put the dough in a lightly oiled bowl. Cover with lightly oiled cling film and leave for about 8 hours (or overnight) or until doubled in size. Tip it out onto a lightly floured work surface and fold the ends into the middle as if you are folding a pillowcase. Repeat this a second time.

Shape the dough into a round loaf and put it into a flour-dusted proving basket, or you could use a colander lined with a clean kitchen towel liberally dusted with flour. Cover with lightly oiled cling film and leave to prove for about 3 hours or until almost doubled in size.

Put the dough on a lightly oiled and floured baking tray. Dust the top of the loaf with flour and slash a few times with a sharp knife. Leave for 1 hour, then preheat the oven to 230°C/450°F/Gas 8.

Put a baking tin half-filled with just-boiled water in the bottom of the oven. (This will create a steamy atmosphere in the oven and create a loaf with a good rise and crust.) Put the loaf in the oven and bake for 20 minutes, then reduce the oven temperature to 200°C/400°F/Gas 6 and bake for a further 20 minutes until risen and hollow sounding when tapped underneath. Transfer to a wire rack to cool. Enjoy!

Sourdough Starter

Instead of commercial yeast, a sourdough loaf is made with a fermented batter-like starter, which uses yeasts found naturally in the environment and in the flour. A starter is made with a combination of flour and water (bottled or filtered). I've used extra strong white flour here, but you could use rye or spelt flour instead. It needs 6 days to get going, but it will become more active with time – it keeps for years!

To keep a starter "alive", feed it every 4 days with 50g/1¾oz/generous 3 tbsp strong white flour and 50ml/1¾fl oz/generous 3 tbsp tepid spring or filtered water. Stir, cover and keep it in the fridge. Ideally, also feed your starter the day before you intend to bake. If you do not bake regularly you may end up with too much starter, in which case discard some of it (or use to make a pizza base) and continue feeding as instructed above. Stir the starter before use.

PROVENÇAL FOUGASSE

This leaf-shaped flatbread is the French version of focaccia. Once traditionally made at Christmas in Provence, fougasse is now eaten all year round and can be both sweet and savoury, or indeed made without any extra flavourings.

**MAKES 2 LOAVES   PREPARATION TIME: 30 MINUTES, PLUS RISING AND PROVING
COOKING TIME: 35 MINUTES**

2 tsp dried yeast
500g/1lb 2oz/4 cups strong white flour
2 tsp salt
5 tbsp olive oil, plus extra for greasing
and drizzling

4 tsp dried Provençal mixed herbs
4 garlic cloves, sliced
12 cherry tomatoes, halved
sea salt flakes

Put 6 tablespoons tepid water into a bowl and sprinkle the yeast over the top. Stir, then leave for 5 minutes until the yeast dissolves and becomes slightly frothy. Line two large baking sheets with baking paper.

Put the flour and salt into a large mixing bowl, stir until combined, then make a well in the centre. Pour the yeast mixture, oil, herbs and 170ml/5½fl oz/²⁄₃ cup tepid water into the well. Gradually draw in the flour with your hand to make a soft but not too sticky dough. Add extra water, 1 tablespoon at a time, if necessary.

Tip the dough onto a lightly floured work surface and knead for 10 minutes until it forms a smooth, elastic ball of dough. Put the dough in a clean, lightly oiled bowl, cover with a clean kitchen towel and leave for 2 hours or until doubled in size.

Knock back by pressing the dough with your knuckles, then tip it onto a lightly floured work surface. Divide the dough into 2 pieces. Leave to rest for 15 minutes, covered with a kitchen towel. On a lightly floured work surface, use the palm of your hands to flatten each piece into an oval, about 2cm/¾in thick.

Using a small, sharp knife, make evenly spaced diagonal cuts through the dough, making sure you do not cut through the sides or the bottom. Very gently lift the loaf slightly and carefully stretch it to open up the cuts a little. Transfer the flatbreads to the prepared baking sheets. Cover with cling film or a kitchen towel and leave to prove for about 30 minutes, or until almost doubled in thickness.

Meanwhile, preheat the oven to 190°C/375°F/Gas 5. Press the garlic into the shaped dough and top with the tomatoes. Drizzle olive oil over the top and scatter with sea salt. Bake for 30–35 minutes until golden and hollow sounding when tapped underneath. Transfer the loaves to wire racks to cool. Serve warm or at room temperature.

RED ONION & GRUYÈRE FOCACCIA

This light Italian bread is enriched with olive oil and in this recipe is topped with red onion, Gruyère cheese and sprigs of thyme. It can also be made simply with a sprinkling of sea salt flakes and a drizzling of extra virgin olive oil.

MAKES 1 LOAF   PREPARATION TIME: 10 MINUTES PLUS OVERNIGHT STANDING; DOUGH 35 MINUTES, PLUS RISING AND PROVING   COOKING TIME: 40 MINUTES

STARTER:
½ tsp dried yeast
125g/4½ oz/1 cup strong white flour

DOUGH:
1 tsp dried yeast
375g/13oz/3 cups strong white flour,
  plus extra for dusting
2 tsp salt
3 tbsp olive oil, plus extra for greasing
1 tbsp clear honey

TOPPING:
2 red onions, each cut into 8 wedges
100g/3½ oz Gruyère cheese, grated
6 long thyme sprigs
3 tbsp extra virgin olive oil
½ tsp sea salt flakes

To make the starter, sprinkle the yeast into 150ml/5fl oz/scant ⅔ cup tepid water. Stir, then leave for 5 minutes until the yeast dissolves. Add the flour and mix to form a thick batter. Cover with a clean kitchen towel and leave at room temperature overnight or up to 24 hours; it should be a loose, bubbling batter.

To make the dough, sprinkle the yeast into 150ml/5fl oz/scant ⅔ cup tepid water. Stir, then leave for 5 minutes until the yeast dissolves. Mix the flour and salt together in a large mixing bowl. Make a well in the centre and pour in the starter, the yeasted water, olive oil and honey. Gradually draw in the flour with your hand to make a soft but not too sticky dough. Add extra water, 1 tablespoon at a time, if necessary.

Tip the dough onto a lightly floured work surface and knead for 10 minutes until it forms a smooth, elastic ball of dough. Put the dough in a clean, lightly oiled bowl, cover with a clean kitchen towel and leave for 2 hours or until doubled in size.

Knock back by pressing the dough with your knuckles, then tip it onto a lightly floured work surface. Leave to rest for 15 minutes, covered with a kitchen towel. Roll out the dough until about 23cm/9in in diameter.

Put the dough on a lightly oiled large baking sheet and cover with a kitchen towel. Leave to prove for about 40 minutes or until almost doubled in size.

Meanwhile, preheat the oven to 200°C/400°F/Gas 6. To make the topping, press the dough with your fingertips to make indents about 1cm/½in deep. Scatter the onions over the top in an even layer, then sprinkle with the Gruyère, thyme, oil and sea salt. Bake for 30–40 minutes until risen and hollow sounding when tapped underneath. Leave to cool a little on a wire rack and serve cut into wedges.

CRANBERRY & PISTACHIO BISCOTTI

Delicious dipped into a glass of Vin Santo Italian dessert wine or a cup of espresso, these double-baked Italian biscuits will keep for up to 3 months in an airtight container. You could try using chopped dried apricots, figs or sour cherries in place of the cranberries, if preferred.

**MAKES ABOUT 28   PREPARATION TIME: 20 MINUTES, PLUS COOLING
COOKING TIME: 1 HOUR**

300g/10½ oz/scant 2½ cups plain flour,
   plus extra for dusting
1 tsp baking powder
1 tsp ground cinnamon
185g/6½ oz/heaped ¾ cup caster sugar
3 eggs, lightly beaten

2 tsp vanilla bean paste
85g/3oz/⅔ cup dried cranberries
100g/3½ oz/⅔ cup unsalted shelled
   pistachios, halved, or a mixture of
   pistachios and blanched almonds

Preheat the oven to 180°C/350°F/Gas 4 and line two baking sheets with baking paper.

Sift the flour, baking powder and cinnamon into a mixing bowl and stir in the sugar. Add the eggs and vanilla and mix to a soft dough. Stir in the cranberries and pistachios.

Turn the dough out onto a lightly floured work surface and knead lightly into a ball. Divide into two and roll each half into a 3cm/1¼in diameter log. Put on the prepared baking sheets, about 5cm/2in apart, as they spread slightly. Bake for 30 minutes until firm and light golden. Cool for 10 minutes and reduce the oven temperature to 150°C/300°F/Gas 2.

Using a serrated knife, slice the biscotti on the diagonal into 1cm/½in slices. Put the biscotti on the baking sheets and return to the oven for 15 minutes, then turn the biscotti over and cook for a further 10–15 minutes until golden and crisp. Leave to cool on a wire rack and store in an airtight container.

Vanilla

One of the most evocatively scented and expensive spices in the world, vanilla comes in various guises: as a pod (bean), essence, extract, paste, powder and vanilla sugar. When buying pods, look for plump, shiny black pods and avoid dried, shrivelled ones. Vanilla pod extract is made by macerating vanilla pods in alcohol and water, but make sure it is labelled "pure", since some are made with inferior synthetic vanilla essence. Vanilla bean paste is made from the seeds of the vanilla pod. Conveniently sold in jars, it is considered the next best thing to the pod.

GINGER & CHOCOLATE SHORTBREAD

These biscuits are buttery and crumbly with a slight heat from the stem ginger and delicious pools of melted chocolate – very moreish!

MAKES 10   PREPARATION TIME: 20 MINUTES, PLUS CHILLING
   COOKING TIME: 30 MINUTES

200g/7oz unsalted butter, softened,
   plus extra for greasing
100g/3½ oz/heaped ¾ cup icing sugar
1 tsp vanilla bean paste
a pinch of salt
200g/7oz/scant 1⅔ cups plain flour, sifted
100g/3½ oz/heaped ¾ cup rice flour or
   cornflour, sifted

75g/2½ oz dark chocolate, about
   70% cocoa solids, chopped,
   or chocolate drops
55g/2oz preserved stem ginger in syrup,
   drained and chopped
caster sugar, for dusting

Preheat the oven to 180°C/350°F/Gas 4 and lightly grease a 20cm/8in round loose-bottomed fluted tin with butter.

Using an electric hand whisk, cream the butter and icing sugar until pale and fluffy, then beat in the vanilla, salt and both types of flour. Add the chocolate and ginger and knead lightly until evenly spread throughout the dough.

Press the dough into the prepared tin into an even layer using the back of a spoon, then chill for 30 minutes or until firm.

Score the dough into 10 wedges and bake for 25–30 minutes until light golden and crisp. Remove from the oven, put the tin on a wire rack and leave to cool for 10 minutes. Dust the shortbread with caster sugar, cut into wedges, and leave to cool completely in the tin. Remove the shortbread from the tin and store in an airtight container.

ORANGE & ALMOND CAKE WITH HONEY SYRUP

Reminiscent of the classic Spanish Santiago cake, this light, moist cake has flecks of orange zest, which adds both flavour and colour, and a sticky honey-syrup topping. Serve on its own or with a spoonful of double cream mixed with thick natural yogurt.

**SERVES 10   PREPARATION TIME: 20 MINUTES, PLUS COOLING
COOKING TIME: 1 HOUR 20 MINUTES**

1 orange, about 270g/9½ oz, roughly chopped including skin
50g/1¾ oz unsalted butter, plus extra for greasing
5 eggs at room temperature, separated
175g/6oz/¾ cup caster sugar
165g/5¾oz/1⅓ cups ground almonds

50g/1¾oz/scant ½ cup plain flour
2 tbsp toasted flaked almonds and icing sugar, to decorate

HONEY-SYRUP TOPPING:
juice of 1 large orange
3 tbsp clear honey

Put the orange in a non-reactive pan with 4 tablespoons water. Cover with a lid and simmer the orange over a very low heat for 30 minutes, stirring occasionally to prevent the orange sticking, until the skin has softened and any liquid has evaporated. Transfer to a food processor or blender and finely chop. Alternatively, you can use a knife. Leave the orange to cool.

Preheat the oven to 180°C/350°F/Gas 4 and grease a deep 20cm/8in springform cake tin with butter and line the base of the tin with baking paper. Melt the butter in a small saucepan and leave to cool.

Put the egg whites in a large, grease-free bowl and whisk until they form stiff peaks. Gradually whisk in half the caster sugar, then whisk for 1 minute until glossy.

In a second bowl, whisk the eggs yolks with the remaining sugar for 2 minutes until pale, thickened and creamy. Fold in the orange and melted butter, followed by the ground almonds and flour.

Gently fold in a quarter of the egg whites to loosen the mixture, then fold in the remaining whites with a large metal spoon. Spoon the mixture into the prepared tin and level the top. Bake for 50 minutes until risen and golden and a skewer inserted into the centre comes out clean. If the cake is browning too quickly, cover loosely with foil.

Meanwhile, make the syrup. Strain the orange juice into a small pan and stir in the honey. Bring the mixture to the boil and allow to bubble away for about 10 minutes, or until reduced by half and syrupy.

While the cake is still in the tin, pierce it all over with a skewer. Spoon the syrup over the cake, allowing it to seep into the holes. Leave the cake to cool for 10 minutes in the tin on a wire rack. Run a round-bladed knife around the inside edge of the tin to loosen the cake, then remove the cake from the tin and peel off the paper. Transfer to a wire rack to cool completely. Scatter over the toasted almonds and dust with icing sugar, then serve.

SOUR CHERRY & PECAN CHOCOLATE BROWNIE CAKE

A dense, rich cake with a moist inside and slightly crisp exterior. The cake rises and may crack slightly after baking, but this is all part of its charm.

**MAKE ABOUT 10 SLICES   PREPARATION TIME: 20 MINUTES, PLUS SOAKING
COOKING TIME: 50 MINUTES**

60g/2¼ oz/½ cup dried sour cherries
3 tbsp brandy
115g/4oz unsalted butter, plus extra
   for greasing
225g/8oz dark chocolate, about 70%
   cocoa solids, broken into pieces
225g/8oz/1 cup caster sugar

4 large eggs, separated
4 tbsp plain flour
50g/1¾oz/½ cup shelled pecans,
   toasted and chopped
cocoa powder, for dusting
whipped cream and fresh raspberries,
   to serve (optional)

Soak the cherries in the brandy for 30 minutes.

Preheat the oven to 190°C/375°F/Gas 5 and lightly grease a deep 20cm/8in springform cake tin with butter.

Melt the butter and chocolate in a heatproof bowl placed over a pan of gently simmering water, giving it an occasional stir. Make sure the bottom of the bowl does not touch the water. Carefully remove the bowl from the heat and leave to cool for a couple of minutes.

Stir the sugar into the melted chocolate, then beat in the egg yolks, one at a time, the cherries and brandy and then the flour. Stir in the toasted pecans.

Using an electric hand whisk, whisk the egg whites in a large, grease-free bowl until they form stiff peaks. Gently fold the egg whites into the chocolate mixture in three batches.

Pour the mixture into the prepared tin, smooth the top and bake for 45–50 minutes until risen but still slightly gooey in the centre. Remove from the oven and leave to cool in the tin for 10 minutes, then release the tin and transfer the cake to a wire rack to cool. Dust with cocoa powder before serving with whipped cream and raspberries, if you like.

Simple Raspberry & Apple Jam

This jam takes next to no time to make, which means the raspberries retain their fresh, fruity flavour and vibrant colour. The addition of the pectin-rich apple helps the jam to set.

MAKES 2 X 200G/7OZ JARS   PREPARATION TIME: 10 MINUTES   COOKING TIME: 20 MINUTES

350g/12oz/2 cups raspberries
1 tsp lemon juice
1 apple, about 150g/5½ oz total weight, peeled, cored and grated
225g/8oz/1 cup caster sugar

Put the raspberries and lemon juice in a non-reactive pan over a low heat and simmer until the juices begin to flow. Add the apple and sugar and stir until the sugar dissolves, then increase the heat and bring the mixture to a rapid, rolling boil for 15 minutes or until setting point is reached. Test for a set, either with a sugar thermometer (it should read 110°C/225°F), or put a teaspoonful of the jam onto a cold saucer and leave it to cool for a few minutes. If it wrinkles when you push it with your finger, then it is ready. If not, continue to boil for another 2 minutes or so and retest.

If you prefer a smoother jam, press three-quarters of the mixture through a sterilized sieve to remove the seeds. Spoon the jam into sterilized jars, cover with lids and leave to cool. Store in a dark, cool place for up to 6 months. Keep in the fridge once opened.

VANILLA & WHITE CHOCOLATE DRIZZLE CAKES WITH **RASPBERRY & APPLE JAM**

These individual cakes are a take on the classic Victoria sponge and are topped with a white chocolate icing. Use a silicone muffin tray or a metal muffin tin.

MAKES 12   PREPARATION TIME: 30 MINUTES, PLUS COOLING   COOKING TIME: 20 MINUTES

200g/7oz unsalted butter, softened
200g/7oz/scant 1 cup caster sugar
1 tsp vanilla bean paste
4 eggs
200g/7oz/scant 1⅔ cups plain flour, sifted
1 heaped tsp baking powder

FILLING:
200ml/7fl oz/scant 1 cup double cream
1 tsp vanilla bean paste
60g/2¼ oz Simple Raspberry & Apple Jam (see page 208)

TOPPING:
4 tbsp double cream
40g/1½ oz white chocolate, grated
fresh raspberries

Preheat the oven to 180°C/350°F/Gas 4. If using a metal muffin tin rather than a silicone muffin tray, line it with paper cases. Cream the butter and sugar together until pale and fluffy. Add the vanilla, then add the eggs, one at a time, beating in each before adding the next. Fold in the flour and baking powder.

Spoon the mixture into the muffin tray or into the paper cases in the muffin tin. Bake for 18–20 minutes until risen and light golden. Remove from the oven, put the tin on a wire rack and leave to cool for 5 minutes, then turn out the cakes and leave to cool completely.

Meanwhile, make the topping. Put the cream in a small saucepan and heat to boiling point. Remove the pan from the heat and stir in the white chocolate until melted. Leave to cool until thick enough to drizzle over the cakes.

To make the filling, whisk the cream with the vanilla until it forms soft peaks.

To finish the cakes, slice each one in half crossways and spread one half with 1 teaspoon of the jam and top with a good spoonful of the cream. Sandwich the filling with the other half of sponge. Drizzle the white chocolate icing over each one and top with a raspberry. Leave until the icing has firmed up before serving.

PANFORTE

Traditionally an Italian Christmas cake, this wonderfully sticky concoction of dark chocolate, nuts, dried fruit, spices and honey is so good that it's worth making at any time of the year.

MAKES 16 WEDGES   PREPARATION TIME: 20 MINUTES   COOKING TIME: 40 MINUTES

butter, for greasing
rice paper, for lining (optional)
140g/5oz/1 cup shelled hazelnuts
125g/4½ oz/heaped ¾ cup blanched
   almonds
70g/2½ oz/heaped ½ cup plain flour,
   sifted
1 tbsp cocoa powder
1 heaped tsp mixed spice

100g/3½ oz dried apricots, chopped
80g/2¾ oz dried figs, chopped
125g/4½ oz plain chocolate, about
   70% cocoa solids, chopped
125ml/4fl oz/½ cup clear honey
75g/2½ oz/scant ⅓ cup caster sugar
75g/2½ oz/heaped ⅓ cup soft light
   brown sugar
icing sugar, for dusting

Preheat the oven to 180°C/350°F/Gas 4. Lightly grease a 22cm/8½in springform cake tin with butter and line the base with baking paper. For a more authentic appearance, line the base with a round of edible rice paper.

Put the hazelnuts and almonds on two baking trays and toast in the oven for about 9 minutes, turning once, until starting to colour. Remove from the oven and leave to cool, then chop the nuts in half.

Sift the flour, cocoa powder and mixed spice into a bowl and stir in the dried apricots, figs and toasted nuts.

Put the chocolate, honey and sugar in a heavy-based saucepan and set over a low heat, stirring until the chocolate melts. Pour into the flour mixture and mix well to combine. Spoon the mixture into the tin and working quickly before it sets, spread into an even layer, first with the back of a spoon, then with wet hands.

Bake for 25–30 minutes, or until just firm, and leave to cool in the tin. Remove from the tin, dust with icing sugar and serve cut into wedges.

Dried Fruit

With its intense sweetness, dried fruit is an excellent alternative to sugar and comes with the bonus of being high in fibre and nutritious. You can buy mixed bags, but for cooks who like to include dried fruit in their baking or indeed in savoury dishes, such as curries and tagines, it's a better option to buy fruit separately so you can control the proportions. Always buy unsulphured apricots, which are deep orange in colour and have a wonderful toffee-like taste.

SPICED BAKLAVA

Those with a sweet tooth will love this rich Middle Eastern sweetmeat. This version is made with layers of crisp filo pastry, filled with chopped nuts and sweetened with a lightly spiced rose water syrup.

MAKES ABOUT 34   PREPARATION TIME: 20 MINUTES   COOKING TIME: 1 HOUR

165g/5¾oz unsalted butter, plus extra
   for greasing
20 sheets of filo, each sheet 25 x 20cm/
   10 x 8in
80g/2¾oz/½ cup unsalted shelled
   pistachios, finely chopped
80g/2¾oz/½ cup blanched almonds,
   finely chopped
finely grated zest of 1 orange
2 tbsp granulated sugar

SYRUP:
300g/10½ oz/heaped 1⅓ cups granulated
   sugar
juice of ½ lemon
6 cardamom pods, split
1 tsp ground cinnamon
2 tbsp rose water

Preheat the oven to 170°C/325°F/Gas 3 and lightly grease a 26 x 20cm/10½ x 8in baking tin with butter.

Melt the butter in a saucepan over a low heat. Lay 10 sheets of the filo, one at a time, in the prepared tin and brush each sheet with melted butter before adding the next. Keep the remaining filo covered with a damp kitchen towel to prevent it drying out.

Mix together the nuts, orange zest and sugar and spread the mixture over the filo in an even layer.

Layer the remaining filo on top of the nut mixture, brushing each sheet with butter as before. Using a sharp knife, cut a criss-cross pattern into the top layers of filo to make a diamond pattern.

Bake for 45 minutes until the top is crisp and golden. Leave to cool slightly.

Now make the syrup. Heat 300ml/10½fl oz/scant 1¼ cups water in a small pan with the sugar, lemon juice, cardamom and cinnamon. Stir until the sugar dissolves, then increase the heat and boil until the liquid becomes syrupy; this will take about 15 minutes. Stir in the rose water. Remove the cardamom pods.

Using the cuts as a guide, cut the baklava into diamonds, then pour the syrup over the top, letting it soak into the cuts. Leave to cool, remove from the tin and serve.

FRENCH FRUIT TARTS

These stunning tarts are filled with crème pâtissière and topped with fresh fruit – either choose a mixture of fruit in a range of colours or opt for a single variety. You could make the pastry and filling a day in advance but assemble the tarts just before serving. Instead of the crème pâtissière, a mixture of sweetened mascarpone and crème fraîche is equally delicious.

MAKES 8   PREPARATION TIME: 45 MINUTES, PLUS CHILLING   COOKING TIME: 25 MINUTES

PÂTÉ SUCRÉE:
250g/9oz/2 cups plain flour, sifted, plus
    extra for dusting
a pinch of salt
100g/3½ oz cold unsalted butter, cubed,
    plus extra for greasing
85g/3oz/heaped ⅓ cup caster sugar
1 egg, plus 2 egg yolks, lightly beaten

CRÈME PÂTISSIÈRE:
4 egg yolks
90g/3¼ oz/heaped ⅓ cup caster sugar

50g/1¾oz/scant ½ cup plain flour
350ml/12fl oz/scant 1½ cups whole milk
1 vanilla pod, split lengthways and seeds
    scraped out

TOPPING:
400g/14oz mixed fruit, such as
    raspberries, strawberries, blackberries,
    blueberries, red and white currants,
    hulled and halved, if necessary
6 tbsp redcurrant jelly

To make the pâté sucrée, in a mixing bowl rub together the flour, salt and butter using your fingertips. Stir in the sugar and add the whole egg and 2 egg yolks. Mix with a fork and then your fingers until the dough holds together, but don't overwork it or the pastry will be tough. (This can also be done in a food processor.) Wrap in cling film, flatten into a round and chill for at least 1 hour.

To make the crème pâtissière, put the egg yolks and sugar in a bowl and whisk for about 2 minutes until pale, thickened and creamy. Gradually fold in the flour. Heat the milk and vanilla seeds to just below boiling point. Slowly pour into the egg mixture, whisking well. Return the mixture to the cleaned pan and bring to the boil, stirring to prevent lumps forming. Turn the heat down and simmer for 3 minutes, stirring until it reaches the consistency of a thick custard. Spoon into a bowl and cover the surface with buttered baking paper to stop a skin forming. Chill once cooled.

Lightly grease eight 9cm/3½in loose-bottomed tart tins (or use a large 23cm/9in tart tin with butter). Divide the pastry into 8 pieces and roll out, one piece at a time, on a lightly floured work surface to 12cm/4½in rounds. Line the tins with the pastry, trimming any excess. Chill for 30 minutes.

Preheat the oven to 200°C/400°F/Gas 6. Line each pastry case with baking paper and baking beans and put the tins on a baking tray. Bake for 10 minutes (if you are baking a large tart bake for 25 minutes). Remove the paper and beans and bake for another 5–8 minutes until the pastry is golden and cooked. Leave to cool, then remove the pastry cases from the tins.

Fill the pastry cases with the crème pâtissière and arrange the fruit on top. Gently heat the redcurrant jelly with 1 tablespoon water, stirring until it melts. Leave to cool slightly, then brush the glaze over the fruit.

Rich Home-made Ricotta

Making ricotta is not as challenging as it sounds and this version of the Italian soft cheese is wonderfully rich, creamy and indulgent. The taste will depend on the quality of the milk and the cream that you use – the best-quality dairy produce will obviously result in a ricotta with a superior flavour and texture.

MAKES 400G/14OZ/GENEROUS 1½ CUPS
PREPARATION TIME: 10 MINUTES, PLUS STANDING   COOKING TIME: 15 MINUTES

875ml/30fl oz/3½ cups whole milk
125ml/4fl oz/½ cup double cream
½ tsp salt
3 tbsp lemon juice

Heat the milk, cream and salt in a large stainless steel saucepan until it reaches 88°C/190°F. Stir the mixture occasionally to prevent it catching on the bottom of the pan.

Remove the pan from the heat and add the lemon juice, then stir gently and slowly a few times and leave the pan to stand for 5 minutes. The milk mixture should start to curdle and separate almost immediately.

Line a sieve with a large square of muslin, folded into three layers, and set it over a bowl. Pour in the milk mixture and leave to stand for at least 1 hour. After 1 hour, you should have a spreadable cheese and after 2 hours, the ricotta will have the texture of soft cream cheese.

Discard the whey in the bowl and transfer the ricotta to a bowl if eating straight away. Alternatively, transfer it to an airtight container and keep in the fridge until ready to use.

APPLE & HONEY TARTS WITH **RICOTTA**

*Nothing beats the classic combination of honey-glazed apples and buttery shortcrust pastry
– unless, of course, it's served with a sweet vanilla ricotta cream!*

MAKES 12   PREPARATION TIME: 30 MINUTES, PLUS CHILLING   COOKING TIME: 30 MINUTES

½ recipe quantity Ricotta (see page 218)
1 tsp vanilla extract
75g/2½ oz/scant ⅓ cup caster sugar
2 eggs, separated
2 small, firm tart apples, peeled, cored
  and thinly sliced crossways
2 tbsp clear honey

PASTRY:
200g/7oz/scant 1⅔ cups plain flour,
  plus extra for dusting
a pinch of salt
1 tsp caster sugar
125g/4½ oz cold unsalted butter, cubed,
  plus extra for greasing

Sift the flour and salt into a mixing bowl, then stir in the sugar. Rub in the butter with your fingertips until the mixture resembles coarse breadcrumbs. Drizzle in up to 2 tablespoons water, stirring with a fork and then your hands to bring the pastry together into a ball. Wrap in cling film and chill for at least 30 minutes.

Preheat the oven to 190°C/375°F/Gas 5. Lightly grease 12 holes of a non-stick deep muffin tin. Roll out the pastry on a lightly floured work surface, then cut out 12 x 10cm/4in rounds. Line the holes of the muffin tin with the pastry so that it reaches just above the edge of each one. Chill until ready to fill the tarts.

Mix together the ricotta, vanilla, sugar and egg yolks in a bowl until smooth and creamy. Whisk the egg whites until they form firm peaks. Gradually fold the egg whites into the ricotta mixture. Spoon 2 heaped tablespoons into each tart case and top with 3–4 apple slices. Bake for 30 minutes until the pastry is light golden, the filling has risen and the apples are tender. Remove and cool for 10 minutes. Prise the tarts out of the tin and put them on a wire rack. Melt the honey in a pan, then brush it over the apples. Serve warm.

INDEX

ACKNOWLEDGMENTS

AUTHOR ACKNOWLEDGMENTS

This book marks the fulfilment of a lifelong ambition, and would not have been possible without the support and encouragement of Grace Cheetham, Nicola Graimes and the dedicated team at Duncan Baird Publishers. I would also like to thank all our customers for their commitment to and belief in The Bay Tree products – it has been a great journey and an enormous pleasure working with such passionate and enthusiastic foodies over the years. I cannot thank everyone enough for this opportunity, and hope that the book will be enjoyed by many for years to come.

PICTURE ACKNOWLEDGMENTS

Key: t = top, **b** = bottom, **l** = left, **r** = right

Page 2 (tr) Vincenzo Lombardo/Corbis; **2 (bl)** View Pictures/Stockfood; **9** Mario Matassa/Alamy; **14-15** Goran Assner/JohnÈr Images/Corbis; **22** Michael Prince/Corbis; **44-45** ac_bnphotos/Getty Images; **46** idp greek collection/Alamy; **60** nobleIMAGES/Alamy; **72-73** Sandro Vannini/Corbis; **88** Randy Faris/Corbis; **94** Matthiola/Alamy; **102-103** vanda woolsey/Alamy; **122** Vibe Images/Alamy; **130-131** Ocean/Corbis; **132** Tim Pannell/Corbis; **142** Image Source/Getty Images; **156** Diane Macdonald/Alamy; **160-161** Richard Nowitz/National Geographic/Getty Images; **166** Jon Arnold/AWL Images/Getty Images; **176** Jacqui Hurst/Corbis; **190-191** Stefan Braun/Stockfood; **208** Mark Bolton/Garden Picture Library/Getty Images; **218** Image Source/Getty Images.